NBC

NUCLEAR, BIOLOGICAL AND CHEMICAL
WARFARE ON THE MODERN BATTLEFIELD

Brassey's Modern Military Equipment
Series Editor: James Marchington

Brassey's *Modern Military Equipment*

NBC

NUCLEAR, BIOLOGICAL AND CHEMICAL
WARFARE ON THE MODERN BATTLEFIELD

John Norris & Will Fowler

Copyright © 1997 Brassey's (UK) Ltd

First English Edition 1997

UK editorial offices: Brassey's, 33 John Street, London WC1N 2AT
UK orders: Marston Book Services, PO Box 269, Abingdon, OX14 4SD

North American orders: Brassey's Inc., PO Box 960, Herndon, VA 22070, USA

John Norris and Will Fowler have asserted their moral right to be identified
as the authors of this work.

Library of Congress Cataloging in Publication Data available

British Library Cataloguing in Publication Data
A catalogue record for this book is available from the British Library

ISBN 1 85753 182 5 Hardcover

Typeset & Designed by Harold Martin & Redman Ltd
Printed in Great Britain by The University Press, Cambridge.

CONTENTS

The authors are grateful to the following groups and individuals for providing information and unstinting support in this project:

Richmond Packaging Ltd. (Winsford); Porton Vaccines (Wiltshire); J&S Franklin Ltd. (London); the British Ministry of Defence; The East German Armed Forces Group (Bruce Rolph, Richard Westaway and Dave Brennan); Military Features and Photos; Stella-Meta Howden Aircontrol; and STI International Ltd. Also, a very special thank you to the Chemical & Biological Defence Establishment at Porton Down who contributed so much photographic material and support.

AFV	Armoured Fighting Vehicle	MLRS	Multiple Launch Rocket System
APC	Armoured Personnel Carrier	MRS	Multiple Rocket System
		Mt	megaton
BAT-TABS	Biological Agent Treatment Tablets Set		
BBC	Bromobenzylcyanide	NAIAD	Nerve Agent Indicator Automatic Detection
		NP	Non-Persistent
CAM	Chemical Agent Monitor		
CEP	Circular Error Probable	PC	Phenylcyclidine
CIS	Commonwealth of Independant States	PDRM	Portable Dose Rate Meter
		PING	Protection, Individual Nerve Gas
		PLCE	Personal Load Carrying Equipment
DPM	Disruptive Pattern Material	PSI	Pounds per Square Inch
EMP	Electromagnetic Pulse	RAD	Radiation Absorbed Dose
ER	Enhanced Radiation	RAF	Royal Air Force
		REM	Roentgen-Equivalent-Man
FAM	Field Alarm Monitor		
FROG	Free Rocket Over Ground	SALT	Strategic Arms Limitation Treaty
		SLBM	Submarine-Launched Ballistic Missile
		START	Strategic Arms Reduction Treaty or Talks
HCN	Hydrogen Cyanide		
		TEL	Transporter Erector Launcher
ICBM	Intercontinental Ballistic Missile		
IMS	Ion-Mobility Spectrometry		
INF	Intermediate Nuclear Forces	USAF	United States Air Force
kg	kilogramme		
kt	kiloton		
lb	pound/s		
LSD	Lysergic Acid Dimethylamide		
m	metre		
MIRV	Multiple Independently Targetable Re-entry Vehicle		

In this Atomic Age in which we live, we have all come to take for granted the benefits of nuclear energy, in the form of cheap electricity. From the beginning it was understood by scientists that nuclear energy could also be released in a massive, uncontrolled burst to create the ultimate weapon of destruction. The German scientist Otto Hahn realised that if atoms of a heavy element, such as uranium, were bombarded with neutrons, the atoms would be split, thereby creating new atoms of a lighter element and releasing more neutrons, which would strike other uranium atoms to create a 'chain reaction' and release a huge burst of energy. He estimated that the resulting force would be equal to the power of 1,000 tons or one kiloton of TNT.

Fortunately for the Allies in the Second World War, the Germans did not develop their own nuclear bomb. Many European scientists had fled to Britain and the USA just before the outbreak of war to avoid persecution by the Nazi regime and only later, when America became a co-belligerent with Britain, did the resources, funds and equipment become available to them to pursue the development of an atomic bomb. A team of top international scientists, including such respected names as Otto Frisch, Niels Bohr, Enrico Fermi and Robert Oppenheimer, was assembled to work on what was code-named the 'Manhattan Project' to develop the first atomic bomb.

On 16 July 1945 at Alamagordo in the New Mexico desert the first atomic device in the world was exploded, creating the explosive force of 20 kilotons. The cryptic message describing its success, code-named 'Trinity', was radioed to the Allied leaders meeting in Potsdam: 'Operated on this morning. Diagnosis not yet complete but results seem satisfactory and already exceed expectations.' On hearing of the news Winston Churchill, the British Prime Minister, turned to the American Secretary of War, Henry Stimson, and said, 'What was gunpowder? Trivial. What was electricity? Meaningless. This Atomic Bomb is the Second Coming in Wrath.'

The Manhattan Project was one of the most closely guarded secrets of the war and its development had cost an estimated $2,000 million. Over the following weeks the world was to learn of the atomic weapon and

A German gas attack on the Eastern front during the First World War, photographed by a Russian aviator

understand that it had entered a new era from which there was no turning back. The same scientists also knew that by generating nuclear energy in a controlled environment it could be made to release energy which could be harnessed to help the human race. Only in the wake of the two nuclear devices ever used in time of war, and the nuclear accidents involving power stations as at Three Mile Island in 1979 in America and Chernobyl in Ukraine in 1986, have we come to understand fully the power which can be released by nuclear devices. We have also come to realise the terrible long-term side effects caused by radioactive fallout.

Unlike most chemical agents, radiation cannot be smelled, tasted or seen. The bombs dropped on Nagasaki and Hiroshima in August 1945 ended the war with Japan, but caused nearly 120,000 casualties instantly. In the many years since that time tens of thousands more have succumbed to long-term radiation sickness. During the First World War, the first of many twentieth-century conflicts in which chemical weapons were used, fairly reliable records of casualties were kept by the Allies and the Central Powers alike. The total number of casualties reported by the major belligerent nations for the three years of war in which gas was used amount to 1,296,853, of which just over 91,000 were fatalities.

Looking back on the First World War, many men recalled the dread fear they had of gas. Norman Gladden stated that poisonous gas attacks 'inspired a fear that was out of all proportion to the damage done'. Another officer claimed that gases were 'damnable' and that it was 'not soldiering to use stuff like that'. Ten years after the war new cases of serious diseases, such as war-gas keratitis (ulceration of the eyes), were still being reported. The historian Dennis Winter in his book *Death's Men* makes the point that an estimated 400 men who were exposed to mustard gas were still alive in 1990. Through the 1930s and on to the present day, chemical agents are still being used – but nowadays their effects are more immediate due to the virulent nature of newly-developed agents which are almost instantaneously lethal. It has been calculated that some 30 agents may be weaponised, ranging from gases to biological agents.

Chemical manufacturing plants around the world have also had their fair share of accidents, such as the Union Carbide plant in 1984 in Bhopal, India and the Seveso plant in Italy. The former incident caused 2,000 immediate deaths and long-term illnesses in a further 20,000 victims. While neither of these plants was involved in producing chemical agents for military purposes, the resulting accidents, which released huge clouds of toxic substances, illustrate how vulnerable an unprotected civilian population would be to chemical attack in time of war.

The exact size of the chemical and biological weapon stockpiles around the world is hard to determine. Estimates vary from the believable to the wildly inaccurate. Outbreaks of diseases may be contained, such as by mass inoculation, but should biological weapons be deployed wholesale, no one would be able to predict what the outcome would be. In fact, disease has always inflicted more casualties than have weapons and this remained so until the First World War. For example, during the Crimean War, the French deployed some 300,000 men, of whom 21,000 died through disease compared to 11,000 in combat. The British fared no better. Of the 111,300 men who served in the Crimea only 4,774 were killed during the fighting but more than 16,000 died from cholera and typhoid. These naturally-occurring diseases were to remain a constant threat to military operations until the beginning of the twentieth century, when medical and sanitary conditions improved dramatically.

In the late 1980s it was estimated that the Soviet stockpile of chemical weapons was about 350,000 tons, while for the Americans a figure of 42,000 tons was released. In 1969 the American stockpile of chemical weapons was believed to include some 700,000 artillery shells, rockets and bombs. In the 1980s the Americans had about 4,700 troops tasked to chemical warfare, while the Soviets had 100,000 troops similarly trained.

To protect troops in the field from the effects of Nuclear, Biological and Chemical (NBC) agents a whole support system has had to be generated. Special protective suits, respirators, decontaminating sprays and medications have been developed to increase the battlefield survivability of troops. Just occasionally even the best prepared army may find itself short of some essential part of its protective infrastructure. Such a case occurred in the US Army in the early 1980s, when it was desperately short of NBC protective suits and had to purchase 200,000 sets of the British Army's Mk.3 suits and boots for its troops in Western Europe.

Nuclear weapons fall into two categories: strategic and tactical. The former group is outside the scope of this book, but encompasses the long-range bomber and the submarine-launched and intercontinental ballistic missiles, which together form the so-called 'triad' of strategic forces. The tactical group of weapons, usually missiles launched from mobile transporters, are classed as battlefield weapons, despite the fact that some of them have ranges of hundreds of kilometres. Such tactical missiles may also be used to deliver chemical and biological agents against enemy forces, and tube and rocket artillery systems may be used for the same purpose. Furthermore, an artillery system of 155mm calibre or greater can also fire specially-developed nuclear shells to a range of only a few miles to inflict localised damage and affect morale.

Such, then, is the range and scope of nuclear, chemical and biological warfare. First one side develops an agent, then the other develops an antidote or countermeasure to it. This 'arms racing' characterised the position between NATO and the Warsaw Pact into the 1980s. With the collapse of the Warsaw Pact in February 1991 the Cold War effectively ended. However, tensions between neighbouring states in other regions regularly escalate into war, such as Iran and Iraq between 1980 and 1988, during which chemical weapons were used. One only hopes that common-sense prevails and that the day of 'Armageddon', the supreme conflict between the nations, as prophesied in The Bible in Revelations 16:16, will never arrive.

American-built *Improved Lance* tactical nuclear missile (never entered service)

Group	Gas	Persistence	Smell	Physical and Chemical Properties
Tear Gas	C.A.P. (Chlor-aceto-phenone)	Non-persistent	Faintly of floor polish	White crystalline solid vaporized when heated
Tear Gas 2a	K.S.K. (Ethyl-iodo-acetate)	Persistent	Peardrops or cellulose acetate	Brown oily liquid in commercial form
Tear Gas	B.B.C. (Bromo-benzyl-cyanide)	Persistent	Watercress	Brown oily liquid
Nose Irritant	D.A.(Di-phenyl-chlor-arsine). D.M. (Di-phenyl-amine-chlor-arsine). D.C.(Di-phenyl-cyano-arsine)	Non-persistent	None	Arsenical crystalline solids which when heated give off an odourless and invisible smoke
Lung Irritant	Chlorine	Non-persistent	Chloride of lime (bleaching powder)	A gas, greenish colour at point of liberation, soluble in water. Rots clothing and corrodes metal
Lung Irritant	Phosgene	Non-persistent	Musty hay or rotten potatoes	Invisible except possibly whitish cloud at point of release or in presence of moisture. Corrodes metals. Rendered less effective by rain
Blood Irritant	Arsine (Arseniuretted hydrogen)	Non-persistent when used as gas	Faintly garlic in high concentrations	Invisible in its gaseous form. In powder form is a greyish white substance (calcium arsenide) resembling calcium carbide
Blister (Vesicants)	Mustard gas (Di-chloro-di-ethyl sulphide)	Persistent	Faint mustard, onions, garlic or horse-radish	A heavy oily liquid almost colourless in the pure state, but a dark brown colour in the commercial state. Readily soluble in fats and spirits. Liquid and vapour both very dangerous although liquid more so than vapour. Has high boiling point (217° C.), and low freezing point (6° C.), therefore very stable. Less than 1% soluble in cold water, hot water is more rapid. Difficult to detect owing to slight smell which is easily masked by other smells
Blister (Vesicants)	Lewisite (Chloro-vinyl-di-chlor-arsine)	Persistent	Strongly and pungently of geraniums	A heavy colourless oily liquid containing arsenic. Rapidly destroyed by water at any temperature. High boiling point (190° C.) and low freezing point (−5° C.)

CLASSIFICATION OF WAR GASES: PHYSICAL AND CHEMICAL

War gases fall under two main headings, persistent and non-persistent. The former are generally liquids, whilst the latter are true gases or poisonous smokes. These are sub-

Effects	Necessary Protection
Immediate pain in eyes, copious flow of tears, spasms of eyelids and irritation of shaved skin 2a	Respirator affords complete protection
As above—and in high concentrations is a respiratory irritant	As above
As for K.S.K.	As above
Slightly delayed (0–5 minutes) causing sneezing, burning pain in chest, nose, throat and mouth. Also mental depression. Symptoms may increase after removal to pure air or after donning respirator	As above
Immediate and progressive effects causing burning sensation in eyes, nose and throat. Extreme irritation of breathing passages and lungs. Possibly lethal due to damage to lungs	As above
Eight to ten times more deadly than chlorine, being a severe lung irritant but less irritant to eyes, throat and nose. Also tear gas. Delayed action	As above
Violent vomiting. Causes blood poisoning	As above
Has a delayed action wherein lies its greatest danger. The presence of mustard vapour in low concentrations may pass unnoticed until damage has been done. Mustard liquid or vapour will rapidly damage the eyes, lungs and exposed parts of the body, the eyes being particularly vulnerable, becoming severely inflamed and causing loss of sight in severe cases, particularly after liquid in the eyes if not removed promptly. Effects on lungs would cause loss of voice and coughing after exposure, possibly progressing to bronchitis, etc., up to twenty-four hours later with perhaps fatal results. Either liquid or vapour will have no immediate effect on the skin, but after two to twenty-four hours, swelling and blistering may appear. Stomach or intestines will be severely damaged by swallowing contaminated food or liquid	Respirator for eyes and lungs. Anti-gas (protective) clothing for skin
Immediate effects by severe irritation of nose, causing either immediate wearing of respirator or withdrawal from atmosphere. Liquid in eyes will cause immediate and permanent injury, and on skin will cause stinging within one minute. Redness and blistering follow much quicker than mustard gas. Blister will contain an arsenical fluid which must be medically evacuated. Vapour on the skin is less effective than mustard vapour	As above

PROPERTIES, EFFECTS, AND MEANS OF IDENTIFICATION
divided according to their effects on the body into tear gases, nose and lung irritants and blister gases. This table gives the main characteristics of most gases likely to be used in warfare.

UNSPLINTERABLE EYEPIECES WITH GELATINE FILM ON THE INSIDE TO PREVENT DIMMING

FACEPIECE OF MOULDED RUBBER

ADJUSTABLE ELASTIC STRAPS

OUTLET VALVE THROUGH WHICH SPEECH IS AUDIBLE

AIR, NOW FREE OF POISON DRAWN INTO MOUTH THROUGH FLEXIBLE TUBE

COTTON AND WIRE GAUZE FILTERS TO FURTHER RETAIN POISONOUS ELEMENT IN THE AIR

FILTER UNIT

ACTIVATED CHARCOAL WHICH ABSORBS AND RETAINS THE GAS AND FUMES

POISON GAS DRAWN IN AT AIR INTAKE VALVE THROUGH GAUZE-COVERED HOLE IN HAVERSACK

HOW THE SERVICE RESPIRATOR WORKS

The Service respirator illustrated in detail above, is designed to withstand the effects of poisonous gases for longer periods than the Civilian Duty and Civilian types. It gives complete protection against all the non-persistent gases, and partial protection against the persistent gases, such as mustard and Lewisite, which affect exposed parts of the body.

How the respirator of the Second World War functioned

HISTORY AND BACKGROUND

The 'mushroom cloud' of the atomic bomb dropped by the B-29 bomber *Enola Gay* on Hiroshima, 6 August 1945; the height of the cloud at this point was 60,000 ft

The Cold War between the United States and the Soviet Union lasted from 1945 until 1989. During those 40-odd years, not a shot was fired in anger between the two superpowers. Yet the threat of nuclear, biological and chemical warfare hung over Europe like the Sword of Damocles.

NATO believed the former Soviet Union was holding vast stocks of chemical agents and strategic and tactical nuclear weapons. In the opinion of Soviet strategists, NATO had as large, if not larger, destructive capability with its stockpile of nuclear and chemical weapons. However, it was their capability in biological agents which remained a terrifyingly unknown quantity for both camps. With typical, indeed chilling, exactness the Soviets designated NBC as 'weapons of mass destruction'. This phrase has been picked up on and is now universally used to refer to all types of nuclear, biological or chemical weaponry.

Chemical agents have been used in limited quantities to achieve mixed results during the many small wars since 1945. The identity of some of the countries employing chemical agents to further their ends is quite surprising. For example, between 1968 and 1974

Portugal employed chemical herbicides against some of its colonies. Technically speaking, defoliants do not constitute direct chemical weapons designed to destroy human life, but their side effects may affect the long-term health of those exposed to them. This has certainly been the case with 'Agent Orange' which was used so widely by the Americans during the Vietnam War that it was almost indiscriminate.

However, it was when the Coalition forces were confronting the Iraqis in Kuwait and southern Iraq in 1990-91 that training in the detection of toxic agents and the protection of personnel reached new intensity as the situation grew more serious. Iraq was known to have a stockpile of chemical weapons, including mustard gas and nerve agents, and to have used them during the war with Iran between 1980 and 1988. Moreover, Iraq also had long-range missiles, in the form of improved *Scuds*, which were capable of hitting Tel Aviv and Riyadh, and a biological warfare weapons programme. This latter capability had been identified by the Israelis and Americans as being located at Salman Pak, and was believed to include cultures of tularaemia *Francisella tularensis*.

This biological agent causes an infectious febrile disease related to plague, but one that does not pass from one human host to another. Instead animal and insect vectors must serve to pass it on to humans. Symptoms include body temperatures reaching 40-60°C. Pneumonia and meningitis may occur. Treatment is fairly standard in the form of antibiotics administered intramuscularly.

In the event, the missiles fired by Iraq against Israel and the Coalition forces were armed with conventional high explosive warheads. But if the missiles had carried a nerve agent, the lethal effect, though localised, would have produced a greater danger than a high explosive warhead. On the other hand, if the warheads had contained biological agents there would have been the appalling prospect of widespread infection, causing panic and heavy casualties in the built-up areas of a city. It has been estimated that in a limited exchange of nuclear weapons the civilian to military casualty rate would be of the order of eight to one. In the event of chemical weapons being used the civilian to military casualty rate increases to 20 to one. This would be largely due to the unprepared state of the civilian population.

2

A chemical or biological attack would create a battlefield wasteland, where humans, who had absorbed the chemicals through the gastric tract, lungs or skin, would be absent but the buildings and the infrastructure would be left intact. An enemy could then take over the territory unopposed, neutralising the effects of the chemicals by the spraying of antidotes. Nuclear weapons, on the other hand, are massively destructive. They not only wipe out civilian and military populations alike, but destroy all in their path.

In the 1980s the Warsaw Pact and NATO forces realised that even the most limited attacks with chemical and biological weapons could prompt an escalation to nuclear attack, and this realisation probably led to the adoption of a 'no first use' policy by both sides in the Cold War.

Of the three types of weapon classed as causing mass destruction, it is arguable whether biological or chemical ones are the oldest. History is full of references to military forces resorting to the use of either of these two forms of warfare. For example, in 600BC it is recorded how Solon, the legist of the Athenians,

American troops decontaminating their hands with fuller's earth on an NBC exercise.

contaminated the River Pleisthenes with the poisonous plant *helleborus*, from which the defenders of the besieged city of Kirrha took their drinking water. The defenders were rendered helpless from the effects of diarrhoea and could not continue the fight. Solon exhibited few qualms at sanctioning such an order.

One of the few reliably confirmed historical uses of biological weapons was at the siege of Caffa in the Crimea in 1346, when the Mongols used siege catapults to hurl plague-ridden corpses into the city in an attempt to infect the besieged population. It was also common practice for retreating armies to indulge in 'scorched earth' tactics, with farms and crops being burned and sources of water being poisoned with the corpses of dead animals or toxic plant extracts.

In the twentieth century chemical and biological weapons have been used at numerous times, from the First World War to the recent Operation DESERT STORM. During the Korean War, 1951-53, UN prisoners of war were coerced by the Chinese into making propaganda broadcasts stating that the UN had used biological weapons against the Korean rice harvest. These statements were without foundation, but gave the Koreans an excuse to justify their poor harvests. It was also alleged that US forces in Korea had used chemical

weapons against the North Korean forces. Again, these claims were made without foundation. During the Crimean War, 1854-56, the British considered the use of burning sulphur against the Russians at Sevastopol in 1855. Ten years later, during the American Civil War, the Federal forces were prepared to use shells filled with liquid chlorine against the Confederates. In the end neither suggestion was implemented. Over a hundred years later, Iraq responded to Iranian offensives in 1984 by releasing clouds of mustard and nerve gas during the protracted Iraq-Iran War.

Biological agents fall into five groups: rickettsiae, bacteria, viruses, fungi and toxins. They may be delivered as aerosols in liquid suspension or powder, in bombs, rockets or artillery, or sprayed from aircraft. Though many are fatal to humans and animals, some simply debilitate their victims for a period. Many bacteria and viruses have an incubation period which can range from a few days to more than two months. This makes them ineffective as weapons in a fast-moving land battle.

Some of the pathogens and toxins have names that are familiar to travellers in the tropics, and the diseases they cause may sometimes be associated with poor personal hygiene and food handling techniques. At other times the presence of rats, fleas, lice and other insects or vermin may produce similar effects. Soldiers and civilians can be protected against some of the more common infections by mass inoculation programmes and instruction in good personal hygiene, which can produce results as effective as protective masks and special clothing. It was the mass inoculation programme instituted by the World Health Organisation which led to the eradication of the smallpox virus, which has a potential use as an agent in biological warfare.

The first group of biological agents, the rickettsiae, produce typhus, scrub typhus, rocky mountain spotted fever and Q or nine mile fever. The bacteria include the agents causing anthrax, bacillary dysentery, undulant fever, cholera, diphtheria, rabbit or deer fly fever, glanders, Whitemore's disease, salmonella and pulmonary tuberculosis. Plague – one of the 'Four Horsemen of the Apocalypse' – comes in four forms: bubonic, pneumonic, septicaemic and sylvatic, of which bubonic is the most common and initially attacks the lymph nodes. The viruses include foot-and-mouth, rinderpest virus, Rift Valley fever, vesicular stomatitis, hog cholera, African swine fever, fowl plague, encephalitis, influenza, yellow fever, dengue fever and hepatitis. The fungi include coccidioides immitis which produces valley or San Joaquin fever, histoplasma capsulatum and nocardia asteroides. Finally there are the toxins produced by microbes, including botulism and staphylococcus.

The delivery of biological agents is a difficult process, largely because these agents are living organisms. Means of delivering them include bombs, artillery shells, sprays and rockets. The first problem is how to fill the projectile and keep the organism alive inside it. Second is the survival of the organism during delivery. Artillery shells could produce too violent an impact either on firing or on detonation at the target area, resulting in the destruction of the agent. Delivery by bomb and rocket does not produce this double shock effect, but the blast to rupture the carrying container may be too powerful and destroy the organism. This leaves spraying from aircraft as the only really effective means of delivering the organisms in a viable state.

Modern chemical agents, that is to say those developed in the present century, fall into two categories: persistent and non-persistent. They may be further divided into five groups: choking, nerve, blister, blood and vomiting. Each of these groups has its own characteristic method of attacking the human target.

The choking gases act by irritating the lower portions of the respiratory system and serve to destroy the delicate membranes of the lungs. This leads to blockage of the air passages and induces death from asphyxiation. The effects of these gases are excruciatingly painful, and death may take several hours to occur. All the while the victim may be conscious of what is happening but unable to save himself.

The nerve gases, or 'G' agents, are anti-cholinesterase agents that work by blocking the enzyme which the body uses to 'switch off' nerve signals after they have done their job. In this way the body is first incapacitated and then poisons itself.

The blistering agents, sometimes referred to as vesicants, include mustard gas. If used in high concentrations they can be absorbed by the body in lethal doses. On contact with the skin mustard gas at first produces mild irritation of the affected part, but this soon develops into blisters which can be incapacitating.

If inhaled the agent will destroy every body tissue it touches, with lethal consequences.

The blood gases are absorbed by inhalation. After inhalation the agent enters the bloodstream where it blocks the supply of oxygen to vital organs, including the brain.

The vomiting gases, or lachrymators, are irritant agents and are lethal only if ingested in massive concentrations or if the victim is particularly susceptible – an asthma sufferer for instance.

Nettle gases are worth mentioning in passing because of their irritant nature to both the external and the internal parts of the body. The effects of these agents, which include dichloroformoxime, have been likened to being thrown naked into a patch of stinging nettles. Nettle gases are non-persistent and are only lethal if massively inhaled, resulting in pulmonary oedema – in lay terms a swelling of the lungs.

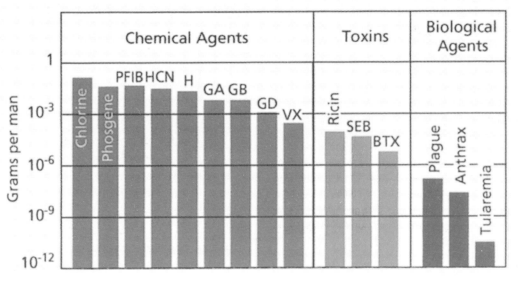

Toxicity of CBW Agents
Inhaled Dose in Grams per Man for Lethality

Chemical agents were first used by the Germans during the First World War when they released a quantity of irritant tear gas in a tactical move against the French at the battle of Neuve Chapelle in October 1914. On the Eastern Front in January 1915 the Germans fired shells containing xylyl bromide against the Russians. The sub-zero conditions at the time caused the gas to freeze, and it did not create widespread damage. On 22 April 1915 the German Army once again used gas on the battlefield. On this occasion they released some 150 tons of chlorine from special cylinders in support of an attack in the Ypres salient. This caused two French divisions to panic, but the attack produced relatively few casualties. Two days later it was the turn of the Canadians to be attacked by gas and by the beginning of May the British were suffering the effects of gas attacks also.

These first attacks produced what was later termed 'gas hysteria' and later attacks invariably provoked fear among those exposed to such agents. The Allies had had ample warning of an impending chemical attack by the Germans but they chose to ignore the signs. Even German prisoners referred to gas but they did not know its composition. A German deserter who appeared in French lines as early as 13 April described the gas apparatus in detail, and was even equipped with his respirator. Still nothing was done. After the war the name of the German deserter, who came from the 11th Division, was published in an article written by the former commander of the unit. The man was subsequently arrested and in 1932 the Reich Supreme Court sentenced him to ten years' imprisonment.

Gas was used by all sides during the First World War, including Italy and America who produced 4,100 and 6,215 tons of gas agents, respectively. The total number of gas casualties recorded in the First World War is of the order of 1.2 million non-fatal injuries and more than 91,000 fatalities, the latter figure accounting for less than two per cent of the war's total casualty list. The USA considered gas to be a major threat to its troops, although fewer than 1,500 American deaths were caused by gas. However, more than 71,000 American troops were injured in gas attacks.

Initially gas was simply released from cylinders by opening release valves and allowing favourable winds to waft it towards the enemy. This very uncertain method

was used by all sides during the war, but later the techniques of loading agents into artillery shells and mortar bombs were perfected. By the end of the war, when one shell in every four fired was filled with gas, it was used as a filling for no fewer than 63 different types of shell. Phosgene followed chlorine and was more effective as a battlefield choking agent since it was harder to detect before it took effect. Choking agents produce an effect called 'dry-land drowning' in which the victim's lungs fill with liquid produced by the body.

Two German chemists, Lommel and Steinkopf, developed a blister agent which was code-named LoSt from their two names, but the British called it mustard gas from its smell and the yellow cross markings on its canister. Mustard gas burns the skin and if inhaled destroys the tissues of the throat and lungs; it may also blind. The first use of mustard gas by the Germans was in July 1917 and in six weeks it had produced 20,000 British casualties. At the close of the First World War Corporal Adolf Hitler was temporarily blinded by the effects of British mustard gas, an event which, it has been argued, influenced him in his decision against using gas in the battles of the Second World War.

During the intervention by the West in the Russian Civil War of 1918-21, British gunners fired mustard gas at Bolshevik troops, in effect waging chemical war against the nascent Soviet Union.

During 1936 a German scientist, Dr Gerhard Schrader, was engaged in developing a range of new pesticides when he made an accidental discovery which would lead to the production of nerve agents. In late December 1936 Schrader sprayed some insects with a solution of one of his new chemicals at a 1:200,000 strength, and succeeded in killing them. Schrader must have contaminated himself because a few weeks later he reported side effects which made him sensitive to light, giddy and produced difficulty in breathing. The effects lasted for at least three weeks.

What Schrader had stumbled on was Tabun (later given the NATO designation GA). Under Nazi decrees he was obliged to report his findings if they were deemed to have military potential. A series of tests on animals confirmed its lethality. Unlike other gases, Tabun did not have to be inhaled: its presence on exposed skin was enough to induce spasms and death. The discovery of

Tabun soon led to the development of the nerve agents Sarin (GB) and Soman (GD) (developed at the close of the war). Captured German nerve agent stocks – estimated to be about 12,000 tons of Tabun – and the processing plant formed the basis of the post-war Soviet chemical weapons programme.

Post-war research produced the V agents (VE, VG and VS) which, like the G agents, upset the balance between the sympathetic (andrenergic) and the parasympathetic (cholinergic) nervous systems which together form the autonomic nervous system. Another German chemist involved in the development of nerve gases was Fritz Haber, who coined the phrase 'a higher form of killing' to describe the effects of gas warfare. In the event and despite advances in chemical warfare and its means of delivery, no chemical attacks were made by either side in the European theatre in the Second World War. Probably the major incident was an accident

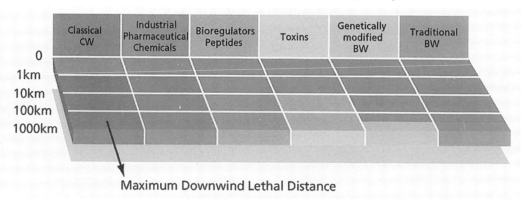

Maximum Downwind Lethal Distance

CBW Threat Spectrum

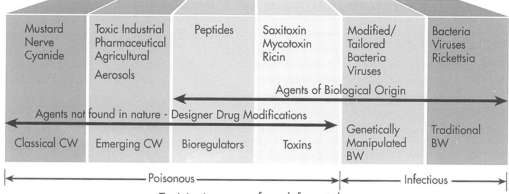

Toxicity increases from left to right

in the southern Italian port of Bari, when a quantity of mustard gas was released from an Allied ship in 1943. The casualty list included more than 1,000 Italian civilians.

Blood agents include hydrogen cyanide or HCN (AC), cyanogen chloride (CK), and arsine (SA). These are absorbed by breathing and affect the enzyme cytochrome oxidase, preventing the normal transfer of blood to body tissue. Vomiting agents include adamsite which was used in the First World War. Probably the best known of all tear agents is chlorobenzalmalononitrile or CS. Others include CN, CNC, CNS, CNB and bromobenzylcyanide or BBC. The tear agents produce a stinging peppery sensation around the eyes and nose and on sweaty skin. Heavy doses can produce a feeling of disorientation.

An unusual group of agents are designated as incapacitating and include BZ and LSD. These do not kill or disable but produce symptoms which include hallucinations and maniacal behaviour. The Americans are known to have conducted experiments with these agents, but due to the unpredictability of their nature do not consider them militarily viable.

Artillery shells, long-range rockets and bombs can be filled with chemical agents. Unlike biological agents these agents are not inactivated by the high pressures associated with firing artillery shells. However, the casing surrounding chemical agents has to contain enough explosive to break it open and disperse the filling. Too much explosive will result in the chemical being burnt off by the blast. Too little explosive will result in only a localised effect.

Long-term stockpiling of chemical weapons has shown them to be unstable. Regular inspections of storage facilities revealed that some types were leaking, the chemical content having perished the seals of the weapons, thus creating a rupture hazard to the handlers. In order to circumvent this a range of chemical weapons known as binary weapons was developed. In essence a binary weapon comprises two parts, each containing a chemical which is relatively safe by itself, but when mixed with the second substance will produce an agent such as Sarin. For example, a typical artillery shell will house the usual fuse and a small explosive burster charge in the nose cone; behind this will be fitted a cylinder containing methylphosphonyl difluoride (DF)

which will be separated from a second cylinder by means of a rupture disc. The second cylinder would contain isopropanol (IP) and a promoter. On detonation, such a weapon would produce 70 per cent GB and 30 per cent hydrogen fluoride, a combination which would certainly render the target area unusable to an enemy. Another binary shell could be constructed to contain ethyl 2-diisopropylaminoethyl methyl phosphonite (QL) and dimethyl polysulphide (NM) which on detonation and mixing together would produce VX nerve gas.

The scale and effects of nuclear war would be likely to dwarf those of chemical attacks, but the mortality rates in biological warfare could eventually become comparable to those of low-level nuclear attacks.

There are four effects from a nuclear explosion: thermal radiation, blast, nuclear radiation and electromagnetic phenomena. The first noticeable effect of thermal radiation is the flash, which has been described by a survivor of the atomic bombs dropped on Japan as being 'brighter than a thousand suns'. After the flash comes an intense heat which produces fires in inflammable buildings and burns unprotected humans. Blast may arise from air-burst nuclear weapons or from surface or sub-surface explosions. According to where they burst, nuclear weapons may produce a crater and throw up radioactive debris, or cause little damage but greater radiation. After the initial radiation produced by a nuclear device comes residual radiation in dust, debris and rain – known as 'fallout'. The Electromagnetic Pulse (EMP) which follows a nuclear explosion lasts for only millionths of a second, but produces thousands of volts per metre over the whole frequency spectrum. This phenomenon has only recently come to be fully understood, but it is known to be capable of destroying electronic and electrical equipment that has not been protected or 'hardened'.

Atomic or nuclear weapons have been used offensively only twice, but the superpowers have been to the brink of using them many times. The use of nuclear weapons was considered by the USA during the overwhelming Chinese offensive in the Korean War. The 'Cuban Missile Crisis' in 1962 brought the superpowers closer to the brink than ever before or since. However, commonsense has prevailed and each side backed away from using the ultimate in mass destruction weapons.

The first atomic device to be used in war was dropped on 6 August 1945 on the Japanese city of Hiroshima. The device, code-named 'Little Boy', was released from a USAAF B-29 aircraft and amazed observers with its destructive power. A total of 78,000 casualties was inflicted and two-thirds of the buildings in the city were destroyed. Three days later, on 9 August,

a second device, code-named 'Fat Man', was dropped from another B-29 bomber on Nagasaki. A Japanese journalist reported on the bombing of Hiroshima:

Beyond the zone of utter death in which nothing remained alive, houses collapsed in a swirl of bricks and girders. Up to about three miles from the centre of the explosion, lightly built houses were flattened as though they had been built of cardboard. Those inside were either killed or, managing to extricate themselves by some miracle, found themselves surrounded by fire. And the few who succeeded in making their way to safety generally died about twenty days later from the delayed effects of the deadly gamma rays.

The bomb on Nagasaki produced 39,000 casualties and destroyed huge areas of the city. This second device was equivalent in strength to 20 kilotons of TNT. It has been calculated that to produce the same destructive effect conventionally, 10,000 Second World War *Lancaster* bombers would have had to drop all their bombs on the same target at the same time.

Since those days, when little was known about the effects of atomic bombs, technology has advanced in leaps and bounds. Through many hundreds of test detonations around the world, much has been learned about these weapons and their effects. The civil defence instruction to 'duck and take cover' in order to survive a nuclear attack is now considered to be hopelessly inadequate.

With the end of the Cold War and the arms control negotiations, including the Strategic Arms Limitations Treaty (SALT) and the Strategic Arms Reduction Treaty (START), between the former Soviet Union and the United States many optimistic commentators thought that the threat of nuclear, biological and chemical warfare was greatly reduced. Both the SALT and the START negotiations covered nuclear weapons, but the matter of reducing chemical and biological weapons had been raised earlier. In 1969 the USA unilaterally renounced and destroyed its stocks of biological weapons. A convention was also drawn up by the United Nations to ban the production and development of biological weapons.

Twenty years later America, under the Bush administration, made the proposal that an 80 per cent reduction of chemical stockpiles be made by both the USA and the Soviet Union. In response, the Soviet Foreign Minister Eduard Shevardnadze called for the total abolition of chemical weapons. President Bush proposed that 'the Soviet Union joins us in cutting chemical weapons to an equal level [80 per cent], and we agree on inspection to verify that stockpiles are destroyed'. In 1987 the US had started its programme to develop new forms of chemical weaponry. There were signs that the Soviet Union was also developing new chemical weapons. However, the Soviets claimed that they had stopped the development and production of chemical weapons and extended an invitation for observers, including scientists and journalists, to visit their chemical weapons site at Shikhany. This was eagerly accepted and the visitors were informed that the Soviet stockpile was of the order of 50,000 tons and could be delivered by no fewer than 45 different methods, including bombs, sprays, artillery shells and rockets. This figure conflicted with Western estimates which put the stockpile at some 300,000 to 400,000 tons.

Fifteen years before this visit, in April 1972, a UN Convention had been signed by 109 countries, including the members of both NATO and the Warsaw Pact. The Convention made provision that the signatories would never in any circumstances develop, stockpile or otherwise acquire or retain:

(1) Microbial or other biological agents, or toxins whatever their origin or method of production, of types and in quantities that have no justification for prophylactic, protective or other peaceful purposes;

(2) Weapons, equipment or means of delivery designed to use such agents or toxins for hostile purposes or in armed conflict.

Such wording would appear to cover any eventuality, but the loophole of 'defensive' research was identified and has been exploited, as will become evident later. As early as 1899 in The Hague a declaration was drawn up to prohibit the use of asphyxiating gases in war; this was followed in 1925 when 118 countries signed the Geneva Protocol, banning the use of gases and bacteriological agents in war. Despite this, Italy used chemical agents against the Ethiopians, and Japan against the Chinese, in the mid to late 1930s.

The technology and techniques of chemical and nuclear design and development are now widely known. Since the break up of the Warsaw Pact, weapons experts from the former Soviet Union are without work and there are indicators to suggest that they are touting their knowledge on a technological black market. This would lead one to conclude that the NBC threat is actually increasing rather than diminishing. Chemical weapons have been referred to as being the equivalent of nuclear weapons for the Third World, because they are inexpensive to develop and do not require the same laboratory facilities as nuclear weapons. With renegade scientists working for a country with even a rudimentary petrochemical industry, it would be possible to create a stockpile of chemical weapons.

A typical example dates from 1983 when Phillips Petroleum in Belgium received an order for 500 tons of thiodiglycol from Iraq. The order was fulfilled like any commercial transaction, and the cargo transported to a manufacturing complex in Samarra, just north of Baghdad. Despite the fact that Iraq was then at war with Iran, the shipment went ahead, because at the time there were no restrictions on the exporting of such chemicals. The Iraqis used the thiodiglycol for the manufacture of **11** mustard gas, which was used heavily over the next five years of the war.

Despite the apparent good intentions of the major world powers, the threat does not simply go away – one cannot disinvent the weapons of mass destruction. At the time of writing, a good few countries are members of the so-called 'Nuclear Club', including the USA, Russia, the United Kingdom, France, China, possibly India and Pakistan, and almost certainly Israel. Nearly twice that number of countries are thought either to possess a nuclear capability, or are likely to have the capability in the near future. At the same time, 12 countries are identified as having a chemical weapon capability, including Iran, Iraq, China, North Korea, South Korea, Syria, Taiwan and Vietnam. A further 18 countries are thought to be seeking a chemical weapon capability, including countries in Asia, Africa and South America.

To compound matters even further, allegations and accusations surrounding the use of chemical and biological weapons abound. For example, between 1979 and 1981 Cuba accused the Americans of using chemical and biological weapons against it. Such accusations were without foundation. Between 1980 and 1982 the Ethiopians were alleged to have used chemical and biological agents against Eritrean secessionists, and the Soviet Union was also accused of using chemical agents against the Afghans.

Israeli troops carry a wounded comrade under NBC conditions on exercise; these men are not fully suited, but Israel takes the threat of NBC warfare seriously.

CHEMICAL AGENTS

DISTILLED MUSTARD

Agent:	Sulphur Mustard
Chemical name:	bis (2-chloroethyl) sulfide
NATO code:	HD
Normal persistency:	Persistent (P)
Protection:	Respirator and full NBC clothing
Rate of action:	Delayed, hours to days, according to temperature
Physiological action:	Blisters, destroys tissue, long-term damage over years
Decontamination:	Bleach slurry, caustic soda or decontaminant chemical agent
Military use:	Damaging blister agent

bis (2-chloroethyl) sulfide

Distilled Mustard

HD

Standard NATO agreement (STANAG) code: HD

Chemical name: bis (2-chloroethyl) sulfide
Common name: distilled mustard*
Formula: $Cl(CH_2)_2S(CH_2)_2Cl$

Family: casualty agent
Type: blister agent (mustard)

An amber brown liquid with an odor similar to that of burning garlic, the odor becoming more pronounced with impurities in the solution. Creates a low-laying color-less vapor around the splashed liquid.

* during WWI HD was variously known as HS (Britain), das Lost (Germany), and Yprite (France). International codes became standardized by convention after 1919-1920.

14 Chemical composition of distilled mustard gas

Distilled mustard is a by-product of the dye industry and its toxic effects were known as far back as the late 1880s. It was first unleashed as a weapon by the Germans in the First World War, who directed it against the British positions in the Ypres sector at precisely 10 pm on 12 July 1917. A mixture of high explosive and mustard gas was fired and by the following morning British casualties began to mount. Mustard gas was so named from its smell, which was described as being like garlic or mustard; the Germans called it LoSt after the two chemists who developed it, while the French termed it Yprite after the location in which it was used. The British termed it HS which the troops, with black military humour, declared stood for 'Hun Stuff'. In the last 18 months of the war it was responsible for 16 per cent of all casualties. Vera Brittain was a writer who served as a nurse during the First World War and wrote the *Testament* trilogy. On observing troops gassed by mustard she wrote:

I wish those people who write so glibly about this being a holy war could see a case of mustard gas...could see the poor things burnt and blistered all over with great mustard-coloured suppurating blisters with blind eyes all sticky...and stuck together, and always fighting for breath, with voices a mere whisper, say that their throats are closing and they know they will choke.

Work continued on variants of HD after the war and it was used by several countries during their colonial wars in the 1920s and 1930s, including Britain in Afghanistan, Italy in Ethiopia, and Japan in China. With typical German precision their scientists developed two types of mustard gas: Sommer-LoSt for warm climates and Winter-LoSt for cold conditions. This was because mustard is not a true gas but a brown, oily liquid which vaporises, and its toxicity is affected by temperature. For example, at very low temperatures mustard will lie in a virtually inert state in the ground and only when warm conditions prevail will it evaporate. Such conditions were not uncommon in the First World War when men would enter dug-outs with partially frozen mud containing mustard gas on their boots. As the temperature in the shelter rose, so the mustard would become active and become sufficiently concentrated to affect the inhabitants.

In the Second World War the SS *John Harvey* was sunk in a German air raid on Bari in Italy and her cargo of 2,000 M47A1 bombs – containing a total of 100 tons of HD – drenched the harbour causing 630 serious military casualties and over a thousand Italian civilian casualties, many of whom died in a few days.

Mustard gas was used by the Iraqis against Iranian Revolutionary Guards during the Gulf War in the 1980s. The use of mustard gas was not restricted to purely military targets. For example, the town of Halabja, in north-eastern Iraq, was captured by the Iranians. The town had a population of some 60,000, mainly Kurdish in origin. A few days later Iraqi aircraft overflew the area and dropped a mixture of chemical and nerve agents on the town, including mustard gas. Some 5,000 people died in the attack, of which one witness reported: 'Bodies lie in the dirt streets or sprawled in the rooms and courtyards of the deserted villas, preserved at the moment of death in a modern version of the disaster that struck Pompeii.' Because of this highly reported use it was considered probable that Iraq had a considerable stockpile of mustard gas which it would use during wartime. As such, this agent remained a primary threat

Large blisters caused by mustard gas

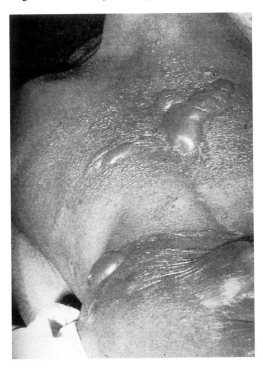

to the Coalition forces deployed during the Gulf War of 1990-91.

HD is highly corrosive to human tissue and if not decontaminated quickly the reddened skin will ulcerate into watery boils within four to six hours. If the blisters are broken they reform and complicate the victim's condition. Prolonged exposure may lead to internal inflammation and blistering of the throat and lungs producing 'dry-land drowning' from a clogged respiratory system. Absorption into the blood results in white blood cell destruction and prolonged exposure causes bone marrow destruction and damage to the immune system. The mucous membranes (eyes, mouth and nose), and areas with sweaty open pores such as the armpits, genitalia and crotch are particularly vulnerable to attack by HD.

As a persistent agent HD may be used to deny an area to unprotected troops for up to a month in wintry conditions. Post-mortem examination of mustard gas victims in the First World War revealed that the entire respiratory system could be clogged with a 'yellowish mucus' and the 'bronchi contained abundant pus'. When the chest cavity was exposed during the post-mortem procedure attendants could be affected by residual gas remaining in the lungs of the victim and they reported streaming eyes and a tightness of the chest. These post-exposure side effects remain a constant problem for medical staff even today when treating victims. This was evident during the Iraq-Iran War when victims of chemical warfare were treated in confined spaces and medical personnel reported symptoms similar to those arising from direct exposure to the gas.

LEWISITE

Agent:	Lewisite
Chemical name:	2-chlorovinyldichloroarsine
NATO code:	L
Normal persistency:	Persistent
Protection:	Respirator and full NBC clothing
Rate of action:	Rapid
Physiological action:	As for HD; may cause systemic arsenic poisoning
Decontamination:	Bleach slurry, strong oxidisers, live steam
Military use:	Damaging blister agent

Lewisite

Standard NATO agreement (STANAG) code: L

Chemical name: dichloro (2-chlorovinyl) arsine

Common name: Lewisite

Formula: ClCH:CHAsCl$_2$

Family: casualty agent

Type: blister agent (arsenical)

A light amber brown liquid with a colorless vapor smelling like fresh-cut geraniums. The vapors cause immediate pain to the eyes and nasal membranes.

Chemical composition of Lewisite

The persistent agent Lewisite is named after its inventor Dr W. Lee Lewis who headed a team at the Catholic University, Washington DC, in 1918. He drew on the results of German chemical agents used in the field to produce a semi-persistent blister agent which has proved one of the most prolifically manufactured agents and second only to HD. At the Edgewood Arsenal the US Chemical Corps worked fast and 150 tons of Lewisite were on their way to France when the war ended in November 1918. Lewisite is termed a vesicant agent but is more rapidly acting than mustard gas, being fatal after only one or two minutes of exposure to concentrations of 500 parts per ten million. Experiments proved it to produce 'immediate excruciating pain upon striking the eye, a stinging pain in the skin, and sneezing, coughing, pain and tightness in the chest on inhalation, often accompanied by nausea and vomiting'.

After the First World War all the major powers began manufacturing Lewisite since it could easily be made by a country with a pesticide industry. For example, in 1934 Japan was manufacturing up to one ton of Lewisite a week and by 1937 this had doubled. It was used against the Chinese by the Japanese in 1934 and by the Italians, who at one time were reported as being capable of

producing five tons of Lewisite per day, against the Ethiopians in 1935.

One of the advantages in using Lewisite is its absolute non-inflammability, which makes it perfectly suited to aerial delivery in spray form. In the post-Second World War period the Soviets developed a range of artillery shells, land mines and bombs which could be used to release Lewisite on the battlefield.

Lewisite attacks human tissue, and in a pure liquid form will cause blindness. Internal injuries may include immediate destruction of lung tissue and systemic blood poisoning (including destruction of both red and T-cells, and cytochrome oxidase) should it enter through the lungs or open wounds. As with HD, blistering may take up to 13 hours to develop, but the action is only a symptom of subcutaneous cell destruction. Inhalation results in death within ten minutes; the lungs and throat fill with mucus, blood and dead tissue causing asphyxiation. The human body does not naturally detoxify Lewisite and effects may be cumulative.

So persistent is Lewisite that it will last for months in wintry conditions and being seven times as heavy as air will collect at the bottom of trenches, sewers and basements. A secondary effect of Lewisite is that it can break down and penetrate many types of rubber, which makes it effective against field equipment and renders some types of protective rubber boots and gloves ineffective.

HYDROGEN CYANIDE

Agent:	Hydrogen cyanide
Chemical name:	Hydrogen cyanide, hydrocyanic acid
NATO code:	AC
Normal persistency:	Non-persistent (NP)
Protection:	Respirator in open areas, NBC clothing if liquid is present in confined areas
Rate of action:	Very rapid
Physiological action:	Interferes with use of oxygen by body tissues, accelerates breathing rate
Decontamination:	None needed in field
Military use:	Rapid action lethal blood agent

Cyanide is one of the oldest poisons in the world. Pure cyanide processes were developed in the nineteenth century in Germany and France as a means of fixing nitrogen compounds from fertilisers for use in explosives. Experiments were conducted with cyanide during the First World War but it was found to be too unstable. However, if cyanide was diluted in water or water and ether as prussic acid it was ideal for use as either a spray or in projectiles which did not contain a bursting charge. Cyanide-based pesticides included the pre-war German product Zyklon-B developed by Dr Brune Tesch. This highly lethal agent consisted of hydrogen cyanide stabilised in oxalic acid in crystalline form, which on contact with air allowed the crystals to produce hydrogen cyanide gas. The Nazis first tested it in the T-4 euthanasia programme in 1939 and later on Soviet prisoners of war at Auschwitz in 1941. Thereafter it was used in all the main extermination camps and was responsible for several million deaths.

Hydrogen cyanide is lighter than air and therefore of limited use as a military agent. In current military use it is used in the form of hydrocyanic acid. Had war broken out in Europe during the Cold War years, it is understood that NATO would have deployed the agent in spray form, while the Warsaw Pact would have delivered it by means of rocket munitions such as the BM21. When descending in vapour form over a troop position AC poses two threats, the toxicological and the explosive. In this state gunfire or an electrical spark could cause it to detonate, producing an effect not dissimilar to fuel-air explosives.

At low concentrations AC causes weakness, headache, disorientation, nausea and vomiting. Increasing dosage produces loss of consciousness, an end to respiration and death within 15 minutes. An immediate lethal dosage will commonly cause a violent contraction of the blood vessels, accompanied by severe shock, which in itself may cause death before asphyxiation occurs.

An attack with hydrogen cyanide will necessitate the replacing of respirator filters because the level of contamination may be so great. An interview between a British Army officer and James Adams, author of *Trading In Death; The Modern Arms Race,* published in 1991, reveals that 'We would find it very inhibiting. Two or three breaths and it's curtains.'

Both the French and the British employed hydrocyanic acid in 1916 during the First World War. It was observed to be immediately fatal after only a few seconds if a man was exposed to concentrations of 5,000 parts per 10 million. During the Second World War the Americans issued their secret agents with cyanide pills, 'L' pills, which they were to ingest if captured, to prevent interrogation. Unfortunately, when taken in this form cyanide produces painful death-throes which may last for several minutes.

The Iraqis are also known to have used hydrogen cyanide gas against Kurdish minorities during their war against Iran, inflicting heavy casualties against unprotected civilians. An even more recent use of cyanide gas was by the Japanese quasi-religious cult of Aum Shinrikyo, who released quantities of it against passengers on the Tokyo underground system on at least two occasions.

PHOSGENE

Agent:	Phosgene
Chemical name:	Carbonyl chloride
NATO code:	CG
Normal persistency:	NP
Protection:	Respirator in open areas
Rate of action:	Immediate to a few hours
Physiological action:	Damages lung lining, floods lungs to produce 'dry-land drowning'
Decontamination:	None needed in field
Military use:	Delayed-action lethal choking agent

Phosgene was first used in the dye industry in the late nineteenth century, before it came to prominence as a mass poisoning agent. Because of this close association with the textile industry, some less-than-scrupulous nations have masked phosgene manufacture with the excuse that their chemical imports are for a domestic dyeing industry. This problem also exists with the chemicals for pesticides which form the precursors of nerve agents.

The first recorded use of phosgene was in the early hours of 19 December 1915 when the Germans released it against British positions in the Ypres sector. The attack inflicted 1,069 casualties of which 116 were fatal. It took two days before casualties suffering from pulmonary oedema flooded British clearing stations. Within one year of this first attack the British were manufacturing supplies of phosgene gas at Porton Down on Salisbury Plain. It was filled into artillery shells in time for British gunners **17**

Phosgene

$$Cl - C = O$$
$$|$$
$$Cl$$

CG

Chemical composition of phosgene

to fire it during barrages in the Second Battle of the Somme in June 1916. By some estimates over 80 per cent of all chemical agent fatalities in the First World War were caused by phosgene.

This agent will incapacitate a man within a few seconds if exposed to 100 parts per 10 million. Fatalities occur if he is exposed to concentrations of 200 parts per 10 million for one or two minutes. Wilfred Owen's poem *Dulce Et Decorum Est* grimly describes a man dying from so-called 'dry-land drowning':

He plunges at me, guttering, choking, drowning...
If you could hear, at every jolt, the blood
Come gargling from the froth-corrupted lungs,
Obscene as cancer, bitter as the cud

Phosgene is the ultimate gas agent, killing not only humans but also insects and mammals, in fact every breathing thing. No wonder such chemically-induced destruction led to gas being referred to as 'frightfulness' by soldier and civilian alike. Phosgene is relatively easy

to manufacture, being prepared from chlorine and carbon or carbon monoxide and nitrosyl chloride under pressure.

Phosgene attacks the lung capillaries and then the membranes of the lung sacs, causing them to flood with watery fluids. Phosgene has been referred to as a lung corrosive which: 'breaks down the tissue into a fatty pulp, thus causing eventual [inevitable] asphyxiation'. Following exposure, death may follow within hours or up to a day. Phosgene is particularly dangerous because it does not detoxify naturally, has a cumulative effect on its victims and may persist in sheltered areas and buildings.

It was one of the chemical agents stockpiled by both the USA, at sites such as Rock Mountain Arsenal, Colorado, and the Soviets. Britain took the unilateral, indeed bold, step of destroying its stocks of phosgene after The Second World War. The Egyptians are more recent users of phosgene, using Soviet supplied stocks against Royalist forces during the four-year-long civil war in Yemen. The gas was reported as having the charcteristic odour of new mown hay, which in itself is not unpleasant, and its use permitted the Egyptians to overrun Royalist positions when all other measures had failed. The use of this agent had the effect of psychologically undermining civilian morale.

CHLORINE

Chlorine is in the same category of agents as phosgene and was used for the first time in a military offensive in 1915. In concentrations of 1,000 parts per million it will incapacitate after a few seconds' exposure and kill after two or three minutes. This is done by destroying the alveoli of the lungs and smaller bronchial tubes preventing the victim from absorbing oxygen and causing 'dry-land drowning'. By the end of the First World War chlorine had been used by Germany, France and Great Britain.

An interesting experiment into the lethality of chlorine involved testing it against the camels of the Imperial Camel Corps. It is recorded how a sickly beast was selected for the trial. The gas was released and the camel enveloped in it, which, when it dispersed, revealed the camel to be contentedly eating fodder. Its constitution was more resistant to the gas than the respirators of the time.

Animals were at much the same risk from gas as humans. Between 1916 and 1918 the British Army reported 2,200 horses gassed, of which only 211 actually died. Special respirators were developed for horses, but it appears that the horses frequently believed they were being fed – there are a number of reports of animals munching their way through the protective equipment. During the Second World War between 15,000 and 20,000 animals were subjected to experiments using chemical agents.

Chlorine, as used in the First World War, was not considered very efficient and in low concentrations it was observed that even rudimentary protection would prevent a man from succumbing to its full effects. However, its use during an attack was enough to spark off 'gas hysteria', as in the use of it by the British against German positions near Fricourt on 26 June 1916. The German diaries record how 'Clouds of chlorine gas...reached the position and being heavier than air, filled every crevice on the ground. The dense fumes crept like live things down the steps of deep dug-outs, filling them with poison until sprayers negatived their effect.'

TABUN

Agent:	Tabun
Chemical name:	ethyl N, N-dimethyl phosphoramicocyanate
NATO code:	GA
Normal persistency:	Fairly persistent
Protection:	Respirator and full NBC clothing
Rate of action:	Very rapid
Physiological action:	Interferes with nervous system leading to muscular paralysis and cessation of breathing
Decontamination:	Bleach slurry, alkali solutions or decontamination chemical agent
Military use:	Rapidly acting lethal nerve agent

dimethylphosphoramidocyanidate acid, ethyl ester

Tabun

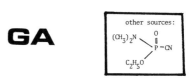

GA

Tabun was isolated in January 1937 by Dr Gerhard Schrader while he was engaged on research into new pesticides for IG Farben. In a lapse of attention, a droplet which had splashed on to a bench during an earlier experiment caused Schrader and his team to develop contracted pupils, dizziness and acute difficulty in breathing. Schrader and some staff were sick for three weeks following the exposure. Controlled tests on laboratory animals showed that death could occur within 20 minutes of exposure. Later experiments with Tabun were conducted on the inmates of some death camps.

As a pesticide Tabun was unsuitable, but as a potential weapon for the military it would have far-reaching implications. A Reich Ordnance of 1935 required all studies of toxic substances to be passed to the government, and in compliance Schrader reported to Dr Colonel Rudriger at the *Wehrmacht* chemical laboratory at Berlin Spandau. Within a year Tabun was adopted as a war agent and the first nerve gas went into production at Elberfeld in the Ruhr. In 1940 production was transferred to Dyhernfurth-am-Oder near Breslau.

Manufacture of Tabun must be conducted under the strictest conditions, with high-speed ventilation and atmospheric filtration. Tabun was formed by the interaction of dimethylamidophosphoryl dichloride and sodium cyanide in the presence of cyanide. Among the

Standard NATO agreement (STANAG) code: GA

Chemical name: ethyl N,N-dimethyl phosphoramicocyanidate
Common name: tabun, GA
Formula: $C_2H_5OP(O)(CN)N(CH_3)_2$

Family: casualty agent
Type: nerve agent

A pale to dark amber liquid giving off a colorless vapor. Little odor in pure state, gives off a smell like rotting fruit as it oxidizes.

Chemical composition of Tabun nerve gas

names adopted by the Germans as a cover for Tabun was Trilon-83, Trilon being the name of a popular detergent at the time. During the Second World War the plant produced 12,000 tons of Tabun, of which 2,000 tons were filled into shells and 10,000 tons into bombs. The shell cache was hidden at Krappitz in Upper Silesia, and the bombs were stored in old mine shafts in Lausitz and Saxony. With the end of the war in sight, further stocks of Tabun were broken down with alkalis and dumped into the Oder. It is understood that at least one factory was captured intact by Soviet troops, thereby giving them a running start in the chemical arms race. Tabun was tested by the Western allies but in the 1950s it was rejected as a nerve agent in favour of Sarin (GB) which is more powerful.

Tabun, like other nerve agents, is either absorbed through the skin as a liquid or inhaled as a vapour. The effect of a nerve gas is to stimulate the peripheral and central nervous systems so that the muscles in the body overreact. Death follows in minutes. Autopsies of victims of Tabun poisoning show massive congestion of body enzymes and fluids in all major organs.

SARIN

Agent:	Sarin
Chemical name:	isopropyl phosphonofluoridate
NATO code:	GB
Normal persistency:	NP
Protection:	Respirator and full NBC clothing
Rate of action:	Very rapid
Physiological action:	Interferes with nervous system leading to muscular paralysis and cessation of breathing
Decontamination:	Bleach slurry, caustic soda, ammonia with live steam
Military use:	Rapid-action lethal nerve agent

Dr Gerhard Schrader, having given the German Army Tabun, became an employee of the army working at a new facility at Elberfeld in the Ruhr. Here, in 1938, he developed Sarin. Its name is an acronym formed from letters of the development team's names: *S*chrader, *A*mbrose, *R*udriger and van der L*in*de. Tests on laboratory animals in June 1939 at Spandau showed that Sarin was ten times more effective than Tabun. None of the nerve gases was ever used operationally because, it was said, Hitler feared the Allies would retaliate with their own nerve agents; in fact they had none. The Germans' faulty intelligence stemmed from the fact that the respirators being issued to British civilians at the time were found to be defective, and a modification was added to the filtering system. This was mistakenly identified as being an indicator that the British had developed gases comparable in lethality to the Germans' own.

During the closing stages of the Second World War prototype Sarin munitions were captured by the Allies, for whom it came as a nasty surprise. Soviet forces dismantled a Sarin plant at Falkenhagen, south-east of Berlin and shipped it back to the USSR where it helped in the development of their post-war chemical warfare programme. After the war Sarin was also manufactured

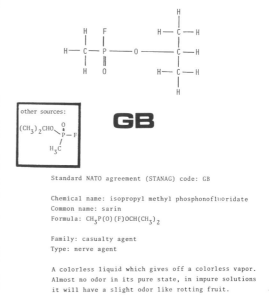

methylphosphonofluoridic acid
1-methylethyl ester

Sarin

other sources:

GB

Standard NATO agreement (STANAG) code: GB

Chemical name: isopropyl methyl phosphonofluoridate
Common name: sarin
Formula: $CH_3P(O)(F)OCH(CH_3)_2$

Family: casualty agent
Type: nerve agent

A colorless liquid which gives off a colorless vapor. Almost no odor in its pure state, in impure solutions it will have a slight odor like rotting fruit.

Chemical composition of Sarin (GB) nerve agent

in Canada, the USA and the UK, and received the NATO designation GB. In the 1950s Britain conducted a protracted series of tests on laboratory animals. The location chosen by Britain as the manufacturing site for nerve agents was Nancekuke in Cornwall, which was not entirely secure and several leaks occurred.

On 20 March 1995 the Japanese sect Aum Shinrikyo attacked commuters on the Tokyo underground using an impure, 'home-made' verson of Sarin developed in the cult's own laboratories. This ultimate in terrorist attacks caused ten deaths and affected more than 5,500 other passengers. Survivors described how they remember a pervading smell which resembled rotting fruit, an indicator associated with impure Sarin. The frightening aspect about these attacks was that they showed to the security forces that some terrorist organisations could manufacture chemical agents for attacking large targets such as airport terminals, shopping centres and office complexes. Follow-up police operations against the group's premises revealed sufficient material to manufacture a further 5.6 tons of Sarin. With such a seizure the Japanese security forces realised that the March attack was not to have **21** been an isolated incident.

When inhaled directly, Sarin causes death within one minute. If it is absorbed through the skin it results in death within ten minutes. The eyes are a particularly vulnerable entry point; therefore donning a respirator is the primary move in protection. Sarin is five times as heavy as air and represents no fire or explosion hazard, which makes it an ideal munition for artillery, rockets or delivery by aerial spray. It is very volatile, which makes it a useful non-persistent agent; in fills for munitions it is thickened with oils or other petroleum products, which could leave low-level residues.

SOMAN

methylphosphonofluoridic acid 1,2,2-trimethylpropyl ester

Soman

GD

other sources:

Standard NATO agreement (STANAG) code: GD

Chemical name: pinacolyl methyl phosphonefluoridate
Common name: soman
Formula: $CH_3P(O)(F)OCH(CH_3)C(CH_3)_3$

Family: casualty agent
Type: nerve agent

A colorless liquid which gives off a colorless vapor. Will have an odor similar to that of rotting fruit, and with impurities may have a camphorlike smell.

Chemical composition of Soman nerve agent

Agent:	Soman
Chemical name:	pinacolylmethyl phosphonofluoridate
NATO code:	GD
Normal persistency:	Semi-persistent
Protection:	Respirator and full NBC clothing
Rate of action:	Very rapid
Physiological action:	Interferes with nervous system leading to muscular paralysis and cessation of breathing
Decontamination:	Bleach slurry, caustic soda, ammonia with live steam
Military use:	Rapid-action lethal nerve agent

Soman was the last of the German nerve agents to be developed. Its name may come from a derivation of the Greek verb to sleep, but it may alternatively come from the Latin stem for the verb to bludgeon. As James A.F. Compton says of the two verbs in his authoritative study *Military Chemical and Biological Agents*, 'both are appropriate'.

Soman combines features of both Sarin and Tabun. It has a lower evaporation rate than Sarin, remaining effective for about a day, which means that air movement will create a down-wind hazard – a cone-shaped plume of the agent blowing away from the point of delivery. Though it requires 30 per cent more exposure than Sarin to have a lethal effect, it is more readily absorbed into the bloodstream and more readily reactive with neural tissue, particularly the brain.

In 1945 the archives on Soman research, which had been stored in a converted mine shaft ten miles east of Berlin, were captured intact by a Soviet task force. Under the direction of a chemical warfare expert, Professor Colonel Kargin, the material was shipped to the Karpov Institute in Moscow. A year later Soman production was under way in the USSR.

Soman prevents the formation of cholinesterase in the neural synapses. The peripheral and central nervous systems stimulate themselves to their own destruction in ten to 15 minutes. This process includes violent muscle activity and malfunctioning of major internal organs. The brain is the most profoundly affected and ceases to function before the bodily convulsions stop. Soman resembles a clear, heavy, solvent or a very light machine oil. It smells initially like over-ripe peaches, but this changes to camphor in time and as the concentration increases. It is less of a hazard to exposed skin in the open, but the eye membrane and any open wounds provide easy passage into the body to inflict rapid death.

Soman is harder to treat medically than Tabun or Sarin, the other G agents. Soman is six and a half times as heavy as air and therefore has a tendency to flow into subterranean field positions, to 'flood' them, and into sewers, tunnels and basements to produce a long-term hazard.

VX

Agent:	VX
Chemical name:	ethyl S-2-diisopropyl aminoethyl methylphosphorothiolate
NATO code:	VX
Normal persistency:	Persistent
Protection:	Respirator and full NBC clothing
Rate of action:	Rapid
Physiological action:	Interferes with nervous system leading to muscular paralysis and cessation of breathing
Decontamination:	Bleach slurry, caustic soda with live steam; flame may be used as a field expedient
Military use:	Nerve agent for denial of ground

While working at the ICI Plant Protection Laboratory Dr Ranajit Ghosh discovered an organophosphate/sulphur compound which was immediately toxic to mammals as well as insects. The research was intended to find a replacement for DDT, but this chemical was clearly far too lethal to employ as a pesticide. Details of the new agent were passed to Porton Down, but since the British were committed to GA and GB the formula was passed on to Canada and the USA.

Somewhere the secret was compromised and details leaked to the GRU, the Soviet military intelligence service and Soviet chemists were able to develop their own version of the agent in 1955 which they designated VR-55. However, it was later discovered that VR-55 was simply a thickened version of the G agent Soman. It was believed that the thickening process involved synthetic polymers and was designed to reduce evaporation and increase the agent's persistency and skin absorption rate.

In the United States a small VX plant was established at Newport, Indiana, in 1960 which could produce about 1,300lb a year. Eight years later 20lb of VX leaked from an aerial spray tank, which was thought to be empty, and drifted across the aptly named Skull

ethyl S-2-diisopropyl aminoethyl methylphosphoro-thiolate

Standard NATO agreement (STANAG) code: VX

Chemical name: ethyl S-2-diisopropyl aminoethyl methylphosphoro-thiolate
Common name: VX
Formula: $(C_2H_5O)(CH_3)(O):(P):SCH_2CH_2N[CH(CH_3)_2]_2$

Family casualty agent
Type: nerve agent

An odorless pale amber liquid similar in appearance to 20-weight motor oil. Gives off a colorless vapor.

Chemical composition of VX nerve agent.

Valley. It drifted over the borders of the Dugway Proving Grounds, Utah, and killed about 6,000 sheep. In 1969 canisters containing VX stored on the Japanese island of Okinawa were found to be leaking and had contaminated several military personnel. This discovery prompted President Nixon to issue an executive order in November of the same year to halt US production and development of chemical weapons.

VX is designed to create casualties through skin absorption or from mist formed by aerial sprays or air-burst rockets or artillery munitions. Within 15 minutes a moderate dose will produce spasmodic symptoms in the victim, including twitching and loss of control of the bowels and bladder. Victims of a heavy dose die quickly; their nervous systems and heart, lungs and brain functions shut down, causing the body to cease functioning.

During the 1950s the British research establishment at Porton Down in Wiltshire conducted a series of experiments into protection against nerve agents. One human guinea pig to volunteer for the trials was a 20-year-old National Serviceman, LAC Ronald Maddison. **23**

One account states that he was subjected to a small dose of Sarin, while another states he was subjected to VX. Whatever the agent was, he immediately went into spasm and died, despite being surrounded by a team of doctors and experts. The incident provides incontrovertible evidence of the efficacy of nerve agents.

In acidic soils VX is highly persistent. It may last for several weeks in temperate climates, which poses some tactical problems. In military operations it would be used to deny the enemy the use of airfields or logistics centres or to seal off the flanks of a fast moving armoured thrust.

In the late 1980s the Americans were understood to be developing a new 'V' Agent, which was designated GB2. The new agent is understood to be non-persistent. The new 'V' Agent would probably be used in binary shells and bombs. The two components in this case would be difluoro (DF) and isopropyl alcohol amine (OPA). Both compounds are toxic, but neither is particularly active on its own. When detonated and allowed to mix, however, these two chemical compounds would combine to produce GB2. A non-persistent agent, GB2 would degrade after a relatively short time and allow attacking forces to move into an affected area.

CS

Agent:	CS (tear gas, pepper gas)
Chemical name:	o-chlorobenzylidene malononitrile
NATO code:	CS
Normal persistency:	NP, but absorbed by porous surfaces
Protection:	Respirator in open, NBC clothing if in direct contact with agent
Rate of action:	Very rapid
Physiological action:	Irritation of eyes, mouth and open pores; non-lethal
Decontamination:	None in open, bathing with strong soap
Military use:	Non-lethal incapacitant

CS gas is without argument the most widely used tear gas in the world, being used by police, military and paramilitary forces to incapacitate and disperse rioters. It was developed at the British Chemical & Biological Defence Establishment at Porton Down following requests for a more effective riot control agent to replace CNS, the agent in use at the time. British forces had found that CNS was not persistent enough and its effects could be defeated by rioters covering their faces with a cloth soaked in either bleach or alcohol.

The team at Porton Down decided to pursue their research back to an agent called CA which had been developed in the 1920s from a non-lethal arsenical vomiting agent developed in the First World War. It was not an easy task, and the team reportedly investigated about a hundred possible agents before settling for CS. The agent is so called after the two American scientists, Carson and Staughton, who first isolated the compound in 1928. However, changes were made to the chemistry of the original substance to make it more persistent.

The first reported British use of CS gas was on Cyprus in the summer of 1958, where it was stated to be highly effective against rioters. By the autumn of that year it had been adopted as the standard agent for NATO.

US forces in Vietnam used high concentrations of CS powder and a 'Mighty Mite' blower to clear deeply-sited Viet Cong tunnel complexes and bunkers by 'soaking' them with CS. During the American involvement in Vietnam hundreds of tons of the agent were used to soften up Viet Cong positions. The British Army and the Royal Ulster Constabulary engaged in internal security operations in Northern Ireland used CS gas against rioters until it was shown that the residual gas which had filtered off the streets into houses was causing respiratory problems for old and infirm residents.

CS is a clear white solid and can be delivered as a powder, which can be incorporated into liquid sprays, or burned to form a white-to-colourless gas. It is extremely irritating to the nose and throat and causes the victim's eyes and nose to run. Nausea, leading to vomiting and shortness of breath, follows contact with CS and the victim feels disorientated. Burning CS produces a vapour which, on contact with sweat, will penetrate through open pores in the crutch, armpits and neck as well as entering through the eyes, mouth and nose, producing a burning sensation in the affected areas. The full effects of CS take about 20 to 60 seconds to occur, and last for about ten minutes after the victim has escaped from the vapour.

In itself CS is not lethal, except in extreme cases where the victim may suffer allergic reactions to inhalation or where it is encountered in such high concentrations that it has displaced the oxygen neccessary to maintain life. CS solids are persistent and the pungent pepper-like smell hangs around training areas long after the use of the agent has ceased.

CS is frequently used to introduce troops to NBC training, where it is employed to show the necessity for respirators and effective decontamination methods. Both authors remember how, during their military training, they were required to enter a chamber filled with CS and walk around while wearing a respirator. The instructor would then indicate for a man to step forward, remove his respirator and state his name, rank and service number in a clear voice. This lasted only a few seconds, but exposed the troops to the effects of CS gas, to give them experience of the real thing.

CS gas is readily absorbed into porous surfaces such as soil, plaster and many organic solids, but is rapidly broken down by the human body.

Agent:	Norepinephrine-acting
Chemical name:	3-Quincuclidinyl benzilate
NATO code:	BZ
Normal persistency:	NP
Protection:	Respirator
Rate of action:	Delayed
Physiological action:	Sedation, intoxication and hallucinations
Decontamination:	None
Military use:	Mental and physical incapacitant

BZ

NOREPINEPHRINE-
ACTING

The incapacitating agent BZ, or 'Buzz' as it was widely known while it was being trialled by NATO, has been removed from NATO inventories, but there are rumours that it was manufactured by the armies of the Soviet Union and the former Yugoslavia, which may have stockpiled it.

Work on non-lethal battlefield agents by the British and the American government in the mid 1950s led them to examine a range of chemicals including mescaline, psilocybin, Lysergic Acid Dimethylamide (LSD) and phenylcyclidine (PC). These psychedelic drugs, along with other compounds such as MLD-41 and ALD-52, produced disturbances in cognition, perception and sometimes behaviour. One drug which attracted attention was 3-Quincuclidinyl which had been developed by the Roche company as Ro 2-3308, and had been identified as being a potent psychoactive chemical. Scientists at the US chemical giant had been working on a new generation of non-barbiturate tranquillisers and antispasmodics. Many of their formulations had the same intoxicating effects and produced hallucinations. The 3-nuclidinyl benzenes had the added advantage that they could be vaporised through thermal grenades in a similar way to smoke or riot control grenades.

BZ was produced by the US Army at the Pine Bluff Arsenal between 1962 and 1964, where it was realised to be ten times more powerful than LSD. BZ is known to be a psychoactive agent, and even the smallest doses may affect the human target for up to 90 hours after exposure. BZ was eventually phased out of the chemical arsenal because its effects on enemy front-line troops would be variable and unpredictable, and NATO philosophy forbade the use of chemical agents against civilian targets.

Standard NATO agreement (STANAG) code: BZ
Chemical name: 3-quinuclidinyl benzilate
Common name: BZ, or "buzz"
Older names/production codes: Ro 2-3308 (La Roche);
    QNB

Type: central nervous system depressant (hallucinogen)

Status: removed from NATO, and NATO member, inventories

BZ is a crystalline solid produced through actions through acetone or ether from 3-quinuclidinol. In its former applications it was used primarily through thermal dispersion, although *never* made in the form of grenades. Production in bulk was for aerial fog dissemination. Vapors colorless with slight benzene smell.

Chemical composition of BZ incapacitating agent

It is reported that the Warsaw Pact saw its application in a different light. BZ would not be used against front-line troops but delivered covertly to command and control centres, where operators would experience vomiting, become lethargic and lose motor co-ordination of the body within an hour of exposure. Continued exposure will produce in the victim a state where he is conscious, but becomes disorientated and incapable of rational thought.

As a vapour it is 11.6 times as heavy as air, and would therefore seep into bunkers and other underground positions where it would remain for some time. It is thought that as BZ took effect on the personnel at these control centres, so they would cease to function in a proper or cohesive manner. The officers and signallers would be sedated and experience vivid hallucinations as a result of which they would begin to involuntarily disrupt and possibly destroy their equipment and, in extreme cases, even attack one another.

BZ stocks have been unilaterally destroyed by

NATO, but it is believed experiments into derivatives of BZ have been conducted whereby the physiological emphasis has been placed on blocking nerve ganglions instead of the psychological effects. It is still unclear whether or not such agents have been stockpiled by the states of the former Warsaw Pact.

BIOLOGICAL AGENTS

If the Germans were leaders in developing chemical agents, then the Japanese were world masters at biological warfare. Very few infectious diseases went unnoticed by them and they systematically set about organising manufacturing centres for biological warfare. In China they had, in effect, an enormous laboratory in which to experiment. In the Pingfan region the Japanese set up no fewer than 18 establishments for biological warfare experiments, each of which had a staff of 300. On their own admission, the Japanese biological warfare research stretched from Harbin to the Dutch East Indies, and from Hokkaido to the Celebes. Among the agents on which they worked the Japanese counted typhus, cholera, tetanus, typhoid, smallpox, tularaemia, glanders and gas gangrene. Each of these agents is highly dangerous in its own right and lethal under the right conditions. One gramme of typhoid released into an untreated water supply will do the same damage as 18kg of cyanide. Other diseases considered by the Japanese as having a military use included botulism, salmonella and 'fungu toxin' which is derived from the livers of blowfish. The Pingfan site was capable of producing 500 million plague-infected fleas per year, such was the level of industrialisation the Japanese introduced into biological warfare research.

New scientific breakthroughs and genetic engineering could make biological agents even more deadly. The Soviets as recently as 1978 were known to be experimenting with Lassa fever, which has an average 35 per cent mortality rate, Ebola fever, which has a 70 per cent mortality rate, and Marburg fever, commonly referred to as 'green monkey disease'. If this is the case, it might well have occurred to some scientific minds to investigate the effects of so-called 'legionnaires' disease', AIDS and possibly rabies. Even the influenza virus can cause great mortality rates. After the First World War an outbreak of influenza in pandemic proportions killed an estimated 20 million people – more than four years of fighting had produced.

By tampering with the genetic material of organisms, it might be possible to create agents which could target specific ethnic groups with particular diseases. Gene splicing to create such 'genetic weapons' raises the issue of whether or not such research is covered by the existing agreements on biological weapons. However, the development of genetic weapons would currently be confined only to those countries where biological research is highly advanced. Nevertheless, despite the indiscriminate nature of biological weapons and the supposed revulsion to their use, it may be safely assumed that stockpiles are held by some countries.

ANTHRAX

Name:	Bacillus anthracis
Former NATO code:	N
Contagious:	No
Normal persistency:	High
Approximate lethality if untreated:	100 per cent
Incubation period:	1 to 2 hours
Duration of illness untreated:	3 to 7 days
Physiological action:	Blackening of skin with malignant pustules
Decontamination:	Live steam or dry heat at 159°C

Anthrax is thought to have been the Fifth Plague of Egypt, the plague upon cattle, as recorded in Exodus 9. The plague of sores, the Sixth Plague, which affected both humans and cattle, is mentioned in the same chapter; this could have been a further outbreak of anthrax or some similar disease such as tularaemia, which is related to the plague virus. A theory has been proposed which suggests that the plague which wiped out great numbers in Europe in the Middle Ages may also have been anthrax.

The bacterium *Bacillus anthracis* was isolated by Casimir Davaine in 1850, and 27 years later Louis Pasteur developed the first major anthrax vaccine. Anthrax as a biological agent with military applications was investigated by the Japanese in the mid 1930s during the Sino-Japanese war as a means of attacking Chinese livestock. The fact that anthrax does not discriminate between human and animal targets meant that it would have killed any mammalian host the spores infected. Indeed, the use of biological weapons may have what has been termed a 'boomerang' effect, infecting friend and foe, civilian and soldier alike.

The theory behind using anthrax in bombs had actually been proposed by the writer Aldous Huxley. In the Second World War the Allies worked on a programme to use it against civilian populations. In 1943 on the small island of Gruinard off the north-west coast of Scotland a device was exploded which released anthrax pseudospores. The test was designed to simulate battlefield concentrations. After the war the island was fire-bombed and burned in an attempt to clean up the contamination. However, it was not until the 1980s that massive treatment of the infected site by concentrations of sea water and formaldehyde reduced the spores to acceptably safe levels. Despite this treatment it was not until the early 1990s that the island was considered safe enough for visits by unprotected people. Winston Churchill was known to be an advocate of the use of anthrax against the Germans in the Second World War. The Allied anthrax (known as agent 'N') project during the war absorbed millions of man-hours, involved hundreds of workers and was immensely costly.

In 1990 as Coalition troops were deploying to the Persian Gulf there was considerable concern that Iraq had developed a biological warfare capability, of which one agent was believed to be anthrax. After the war these fears were confirmed when UN investigators found an extensive anthrax and botulinum research programme which had been under way at Salman Pak since at least 1968. But there was no evidence that such organisms had been put into the warheads of the long-range *Scud* missiles fired against Israel and the Coalition forces' rear areas. A programme of inoculation was undertaken and 8,000 US soldiers received botulinum vaccine and 150,000 were inoculated against anthrax.

Anthrax spores can enter the body through open cuts, or most commonly by inhalation. The ingested form, caused by eating infected meat, is relatively uncommon. The cutaneous form is found among meat packers, and one name for the pulmonary form is 'wool-sorters' disease'. The cutaneous form produces blackening of the skin, swelling and pustules – actions similar to these occur inside the lungs. In its pulmonary form anthrax approaches a mortality rate of almost 100 per cent. What makes anthrax so effective as a military weapon is that, while it does not occur in epidemic form in humans, the spores can remain active and infectious for many years in soil and water and will resist sunlight for several days. In fact, this has led to anthrax being termed the perfect biological weapon.

The anthrax bacillus is only one biological agent of many which has been exploited by the defensive research loophole identified in the 1972 Convention on Biological Weapons, mentioned earlier. In May 1979 US intelligence began to receive reports of leaks from a Soviet chemical manufacturing site at Sverdlovsk in the Urals. The leak had actually started in April, but substantiated reports had taken time to verify. Victims exposed to the leak became ill on the day of exposure and died some days later. The Soviets at first denied any leak but then admitted that some people had suffered intestinal anthrax from ingesting contaminated meat bought on the black market. They gave the casualty list as 66 deaths over a period of weeks. It is now understood that at least 10 kg of anthrax spores were released in the accident and spread three miles downwind. British estimates of the casualties from this incident were in the hundreds, while American estimates put the death toll between 1,000 and 2,000. The Soviets tried to contain the effects of the anthrax by undertaking a massive inoculation programme, but with little effect.

PLAGUE

Full name:	Plague, pulmonary, bubonic
Contagious:	Yes
Approximate lethality if untreated:	Pulmonary 100 per cent; bubonic 50-60 per cent
Incubation period:	Pulmonary 3-4 days; bubonic 2-6 days
Duration of illness untreated:	Pulmonary 2 days; bubonic up to 14 days
Physiological action:	Pulmonary: lungs fill with blood; bubonic: swelling of lymph nodes and formation of buboes

Bubonic plague is spread by fleas, which have been living and breeding on rat hosts which in turn carry the disease. Plague is a zoonosis, that is, it can be transmitted from insect life or animals direct to humans, in the same manner as malaria and rabies. The disease is common to man and animals and thrives in congested urban areas, such as exist in many Third World cities. Among the strains of plague are bubonic, septicaemic and pneumonic.

Bubonic plague is so called because of the visible swelling of the lymph nodes, usually on one side of the body. Individual swellings are called buboes and these contain oxidised blood with dead bacteria which colour them blue to black, hence the name 'Black Death'. The swellings may burst open, becoming massive open sores which can in turn become sites of secondary infection. The buboes may persist for about a week although lessening in size and giving less pain. Victims exposed to bubonic plague can experience secondary complications which can include plague meningitis or secondary pneumonia, leading to shock and respiratory arrest. Survivors of bubonic plague exhibit no after effects.

Septicaemic plague is plague without bubos, and can be confused with lesser bacterial disorders. The victim suffers from fever, malaise and overall weakness and secondary infection. Pneumonic plague is spread from contact between humans where spittle or mucus is exchanged. The bacterium stays alive in mucus long enough to spread disease. It engenders its own form of pathogenic lung congestion or pneumonia. This type develops rapidly, leaving its victims prostrate within hours of onset.

The most notable outbreak of the 'Black Death' was a strain of bubonic plague which affected Europe between 1334 and 1351, and was responsible for killing a quarter of the population. Apart from the black lumps, other symptoms included fever, delirium and severe pain. Death usually occurred within a few days. Other noted outbreaks in the West include the Athens epidemic of 430 BC and the Rome epidemic in AD 262. In London in 1603 there was an outbreak when some 30,000 people are thought to have died, and another outbreak occurred in 1664 which further devastated the population of England. An epidemic spread from Hong Kong to India between 1894 and 1914. An example of how virulent the disease can be is shown in the records of 1665 to 1666, when the Derbyshire village of Eyam was struck. Out of a total population of 350 only 33 survived. This outbreak was only halted in London by the 'Great Fire' which burnt down most of the squalid housing which served as breeding centres for the fleas and rats.

'YELLOW RAIN'

The toxic agent known as 'yellow rain' is a somewhat ambiguous chemical and even today remains something of an enigma. In 1981 it was alleged that Soviet-backed forces were using a toxic agent against anti-Communist forces in south-east Asia. Reports began to filter through to the USA from Hmong tribesmen that aircraft were spraying a fine 'yellowish rain'. Those who came into contact with the substance developed blisters and skin lesions and began to bleed and vomit. The Americans were able to obtain samples from buildings and the surrounding foliage which exhibited the yellow substance. On analysing these, traces of tricothecene toxin were discovered and it was assumed that this was the cause of the reported illnesses. In 1982 samples of the 'yellow rain' were sent to the Chemical Defence Establishment at Porton Down. Here tests concluded that the toxin was no more than a naturally-occurring product from the droppings of wild honey bees.

Today the question of whether or not the Soviets had developed a new toxin for military use still remains unanswered.

CHEMICAL AND BIOLOGICAL DELIVERY SYSTEMS

Chemical agents may be delivered to the battlefield in several ways. First, by tubed artillery firing chemically-filled shells either to disrupt rear echelon areas or deny an area to the enemy. Aerial sprays can deliver agents to targets in much the same way as commercial crop spraying. This might be an accurate means of delivery, but it does leave the spraying aircraft vulnerable to anti-aircraft fire. Free-fall bombs might also be used as a means of delivery; aircraft flying at higher altitudes would be less vulnerable to anti-aircraft fire and larger bombers could deliver greater payloads than, say, helicopters with sprays.

Another method of delivery is the Multiple Rocket System (MRS), such as the Soviet-built BM-21, 9P140, BM-27 and 9A52. A 122mm calibre MRS such as the BM-21 can ripple-fire 40 rounds in only 20 seconds to ranges of 20km. The conventional 19kg high explosive warhead of the rocket can be replaced with chemical agents to saturate an area. The BM-21 system is mounted on either 4x4 or 6x6 trucks which have

operational ranges in excess of 400km. A reload time of ten to 15 minutes makes this somewhat ageing system still a force to be reckoned with. The 220mm calibre BM-27 MRS can also deliver chemical agents out to a range of 40 km. This system is mounted on the ZIL-135 chassis and has 16 rockets in a ready-to-fire position and takes only 15 minutes to reload, which means that a battery of these can quickly saturate an area. The Czech Republic has the RM-70 MRS with a comparable capability.

For its part NATO has the Multiple Launch Rocket System (MLRS), which is configured to fire conventionally-armed warheads on its rockets. Users of this system include the USA, France, Italy, Japan and the UK. Given the technology available to NATO it could,

(right) **Transporter-erector-launcher for firing cruise missiles**

(bottom) **The MLRS can be configured to deliver chemical agents if required**

if necessary, deploy the weapon with chemical warheads.

Like chemical agents, biological agents can be delivered by artillery or rockets in a powder or aerial spray. It is suggested that insect vectors such as female mosquitoes may be used. Unlike chemical agents, however, biological agents can spread and reproduce themselves, leading to the 'boomerang' effect mentioned earlier. Under the right conditions and left unchecked a biological agent can spread to cover an area in excess of 10,000sq km and produce casualties in epidemic proportions.

Post-war experiments using non-toxic, non-persistent agents dispersed in spray form from aircraft have proved how widespread contamination would be over built-up areas. Indeed, it has been calculated that if only 0.077oz of tularaemia virus was released into the atmosphere it would produce a lethal cloud 100m in height and cover a ground area of 500sq m.

The US Army MLRS can be configured to deliver chemical agents

NUCLEAR
WEAPONS

Japanese atomic bomb victims

The first and only employment of nuclear weapons in war has been the dropping of atomic bombs at Hiroshima on 6 August 1945 and at Nagasaki three days later. The Hiroshima and Nagasaki bombs were code-named 'Little Boy' and 'Fat Man', respectively. The first atomic device was dropped from an altitude of 9,455m and detonated at 244m above the target; it had a yield of about 13kt and devastated 13sq km of the city, killing 78,000 people. The yield of the Nagasaki bomb was of the order of 22kt; it killed about 39,000 people and destroyed 6.7 sq km. The damage and casualty levels at this second target were lower because the terrain sheltered many people from the effects of the explosion and the bomb was dropped in the wrong area. Each mission was flown by three B-29 aircraft, one to drop the bomb and two escorts which also carried observers. On the first atomic mission Sergeant George Caron recorded:

Here it comes, the mushroom shape...It's coming this way. It's like a mass of bubbling molasses. The mushroom is spreading out. It's maybe a mile or two wide and half a mile high. It's growing up and up. It's nearly level with us and climbing. It's very black, but there is a purplish tint to the cloud. The base of the mushroom looks like a heavy undercast that is shot through with flames. The city must be below that.

Modern nuclear weapons are divided into tactical and strategic; in the Cold War it was assumed that tactical nuclear weapons would be used in the same way as large-scale conventional weapons. They would be targeted against supply lines, or in conjunction with chemical weapons to blast a gap in NATO defences to open the way for a Warsaw Pact-style blitzkrieg on Western Europe. Strategic weapons would be used to

Cut-away drawing of a typical missile silo housing a strategic Intercontinental Ballistic Missile

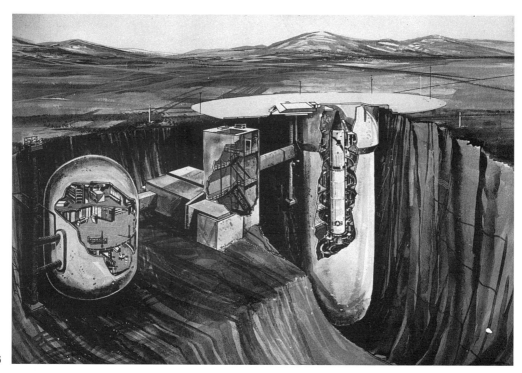

Interior view of the strategic *Titan* II missile silo

strike at military and industrial targets deep inside enemy territory. Initially these weapons were free-fall devices to be delivered by manned bomber aircraft. As missile technology improved and ranges increased, along with advances in guidance, strategic weapons could be delivered as stand-off weapons carried by aircraft, ground-launched as Intercontinental Ballistic Missiles (ICBMs) from specially-built silos or as Submarine-Launched Ballistic Missiles (SLBMs).

Missile technology reached its zenith with the development of Multiple Independently Targetable Re-entry Vehicles (MIRVs) in which one missile could carry several warheads, each directed at a different target. The missile also featured countermeasures to defeat anti-ballistic missile defences such as the Soviet *Galosh* system. Together this structured layering of nuclear deterrence became known as the 'triad' of land, sea and air nuclear capability. This method of organising nuclear weapons allows a country to hit back even if at least two 'arms' of the triad have been rendered non-operational by nuclear strikes. Of the handful of countries with a nuclear weapon capability only the USA, France, Russia (along with some other CIS members) and China have this triad network in place. Britain has an air-deliverable nuclear capability with its *Tornado* aircraft, but relies primarily on SLBMs in the form of the recently introduced *Trident* D5 carried by the new *Trafalgar*-class submarines as its means of strategic deterrence.

A *Minuteman* III strategic ICBM is launched from its silo at the Vandenberg Air Force Base, California; no longer in service, but at the height of its deployment there were 450 missiles in service with the USAF

There are four distinguishing features to a nuclear explosion: blast, heat, radiation and electromagnetic pulse. The first signature of a nuclear detonation is the heat flash which makes up some 35 per cent of the device's energy release, but is only one per cent of the total thermal energy. In the wake of the brilliant blast which generates temperatures of more than a million degrees, comes the blast which may last for several seconds, depending on the size of the device. This blast wave makes up 50 per cent of the weapon's total energy release and a third of the weapon's total power.

Typically, a 1Mt (megaton) device will produce an overpressure of 50psi (Pounds per Square Inch) less than one kilometre from ground zero, the point of detonation. Within seconds the initial thermal pulse is over but the blast continues and will reach speeds in excess of 250km/hr, which will hurl debris to cause widespread damage. The point of detonation by a 1Mt device will leave a crater 400m wide and 43m deep. The heat generated by the device makes up only five per cent of the weapon's destructive power. This might not appear to be particularly large, but when used against built-up areas it could be devastating. If a nuclear device were to be detonated over, say, Birmingham, it could create a firestorm with temperatures up to 800°C at its epicentre, which would destroy everything. The final 10 per cent of a nuclear device's output is made up of radiation, which may have long-term effects and is estimated to produce 15 per cent of the total casualties.

All conventional explosions create a mushroom ball for a few seconds, but the characteristic mushroom-shaped cloud which lingers and boils is the unique signature of a nuclear device.

During the Cold War nuclear weapons were developed which had a very high initial radiation, but since they were designed to be exploded as an airburst they would cause little material damage – they were intended to kill people, but not destroy equipment nor block terrain. These devices, first developed in the 1970s, were known as Enhanced Radiation (ER) weapons, commonly referred to as 'neutron bombs'. A one-kiloton neutron device would produce incapacity within five minutes and death within 24 hours to those exposed to its effects at ranges of less than 500m. The latent lethality zone of such a device was set between 500 and 1,000m, in which case those exposed to its radiation would be expected to die between 48 and 96 hours. Beyond 1,500m the casualties falling into what was termed the 'latent damage zone' would contract cancers and immune deficiency and die a lingering death which could take months.

ER weapons are thermonuclear devices (see below) and typically have a yield of one kiloton or less. Radiation, not blast, is the primary killer. This type of weapon can be fired by an artillery piece or launched on a tactical missile. A 1Mt weapon would produce lethal levels of gamma rays of the order of 1,000 REM (Roentgen-Equivalent-Man) doses out to a range of four kilometres. This would drop rapidly to 100 REM at a range of five kilometres.

One source puts it that a nuclear device kills three times over: by heat, blast and radiation. Of these, radiation is the 'silent' killer in nuclear war. Radiation is measured in RADs, or Radiation Absorbed Doses. Short-term exposure to 1,000 RADs will affect the central nervous system, inflict coma, convulsions and death within days. A level of 800 RADs will induce diarrhoea and vomiting, which in some instances could be confused with conventional shock. Recovery is unlikely and death occurs within three weeks of exposure. With 400 RADs exposure the victim will experience mouth ulcers, loss of teeth and hair, and immune deficiency; death could come after about 30 days. Survival is possible, but unlikely. With exposures of 150 RADs or less the victim could recover with proper treatment after experiencing symptoms of nausea.

The last effect of a nuclear explosion is the EMP which disrupts electrical and electronic equipment unless it has been specially protected or 'hardened'. This phenomenon was particularly noticeable during a high-altitude nuclear test by the Americans over Johnson Island. During the test many street lights in Oahu, in the Hawaiian islands, failed, which led scientists to attach some significance to the effects of nuclear blast on electrical systems. It has since been discovered that EMP spans gamma and neutron radiation and covers a **39** frequency spectrum of several hundred megahertz. Thus an airburst of a nuclear device may destroy power cables, tele-communications and electronic ignition on cars and aircraft. To counter this possibility NATO and Russia have both undertaken a programme of hardening their battlefield communications, radar and data-handling systems.

The largest nuclear device ever detonated was a 70Mt device; before that it was a 58Mt device detonated in the atmosphere by the Soviets in 1963. By a law of physics, which covers both conventional and nuclear explosions, a 10kt device is not ten times as destructive as a 1kt one. Conventional explosives have to be multiplied eight times to be twice as destructive. This rule also applies to nuclear physics, so a device of 10kt will produce only twice the destructive power of a 1kt device.

The first atomic bombs relied on fission to deliver the explosive force, but thermonuclear devices, developed in the 1950s, derive their force from fusion. Nuclear fission works by the splitting of the nuclei of heavy atoms such as uranium or plutonium. To create an explosion using this method a so-called 'critical mass' of one of these elements must be assembled within the device; this is the minimum quantity needed to sustain a 'chain reaction' such that high-energy neutrons released by atomic fissions cannot escape but build up virtually instantaneously in a cascade causing further fissions, the energy from which is released as a nuclear explosion.

Tactical or battlefield nuclear weapons can be delivered as either rockets or artillery shells with a calibre greater than 155mm.

(right) **AS-90 155mm self-propelled gun of the Royal Artillery; artillery systems of this calibre could be used to deliver chemical agents**

(left) **Firing of American *Tomahawk* cruise missile from its Transporter Erector Launcher (TEL)**

(below) **The American M-110 203mm gun can fire either nuclear or chemical-filled shells**

NUCLEAR ARTILLERY

The age of nuclear artillery opened on 25 May 1953 when the Americans fired a 280mm shell from a weapon nicknamed 'Atomic Annie' on the testing ranges at Frenchman's Flat, Nevada. Within the space of a few years, further calibres of artillery had been made nuclear-

41

capable and the Soviets were in the race too.

Today, the Russians still have at least nine artillery systems capable of delivering either nuclear or chemical shells. These include the 122mm calibre D-30, the 152mm 2S19 and the 203mm 2S7. The Americans have several artillery types capable of firing tactical nuclear shells or chemical weapons, including the M-109, the M-110 and the M-198. While not a nuclear power in its own right the former army of Yugoslavia does have the 152mm M-84 towed gun which is capable of firing nuclear and chemical shells out to 27,000m.

The South Africans are thought either to have a limited stockpile of nuclear weapons or are capable of assembling them should the need arise. To this end their towed G-5 and self-propelled G-6 systems, both of 155mm calibre, and capable of firing out to 39,000m, have to be considered capable of delivering tactical nuclear shells or chemical shells.

The British Army does not hold a stockpile of nuclear shells, but their AS-90 self-propelled gun and FH-70 towed gun, both of 155mm calibre, could deliver tactical nuclear shells if necessary. The French 155mm F-3 towed howitzer, capable of firing out to 25,000m must also be considered as capable of delivering nuclear shells.

The French-designed GCT 155mm self-propelled gun could be used to fire chemical-filled shells

The American M-110 203mm gun can fire either nuclear or

chemical-filled shells

(above) **AS-90 self-propelled gun of British design; this weapon could fire nuclear or chemical-filled shells**

(below) **The US Army's *Lance* tactical nuclear missile seen on its transporting vehicle, a modified M-113; *Lance* was also fired from this platform and was a standard battlefield nuclear missile until withdrawn under the Bush administration**

TACTICAL NUCLEAR MISSILES

At the height of the Cold War the Americans fielded two types of tactical nuclear missile, the *Lance* and the *Pershing*. The first was also available to other NATO members in its tactical nuclear strike role. The former Warsaw Pact fielded several types of tactical nuclear missile systems, including the well-known *Scud* and *FROG*.

The proliferation of these nuclear-capable missiles is much harder to contain than nuclear-capable artillery. Many former client states of the Soviets have supplies of *Scud* or *FROG* systems which have been modified and this fact, combined with their nuclear development programmes, makes it only a question of time before these missiles are armed with a nuclear warhead. A missile thus armed, even with a low-yield device, would be sufficient to establish power in a region. The North Koreans are known to have *FROG*-7s, *Scud*-Bs and *Scud*-Cs and an ongoing nuclear and chemical weapons programme. The Chinese are believed to have developed at least three missiles capable of delivering tactical nuclear weapons: the CSS-8/M-7, the CSS-7/M-11 and the CSS-6/M-9. They also possess the CSS-2, but with a range of 2,700km it falls into the category of a short- to intermediate-range ballistic missile. The CSS-8/M-7 has a range of 150km and is also in service with

Iran, a state known to be actively seeking a nuclear capability. The CSS-7/M-11 has a range of 280km and is possibly in service with Pakistan, another state thought to be seeking nuclear status, if it has not already achieved it. The CSS-6/M-9 has a range of 600km and is believed to be in service in Syria. The Israelis have the *Jericho* 1 and *Jericho* 2 systems which have ranges of 650km and 1,500km, respectively. The Israelis are known to have a highly advanced nuclear programme, as revealed by Mordechai Vanunu in the 1980s.

It has been suggested that the potential presence of so many nuclear weapons in the Middle East means that a limited nuclear exchange is not out of the question. Apart from the countries listed here, Taiwan, Yemen, Egypt and the UAE all have similar delivery systems with ranges between 70 and 300km, which can either make them a potential threat to neighbouring states or strengthen their position against a hostile state.

FRENCH SYSTEMS – *PLUTON*

The French tactical nuclear missile system *Pluton* entered service with the Army in 1974, and is capable of carrying a 500kg warhead such as the AN51, which could produce a yield between 15 and 25kt. Technically, France

French *Pluton* tactical nuclear missile system

is not a member state of NATO, having withdrawn in 1966, and as such has to be classed as being an independent nuclear state. Indeed, the French developed their own nuclear triad with little outside assistance. Their S3 IRBMs were based on the Plateau d'Albion, their nuclear submarines were not subject to NATO commands and their air force had its own nuclear weaponry. The *Pluton* system is also a result of this breakaway. It is carried on the modified chassis of an AMX-30 main battle tank and forms the pre-strategic weapon of the French Army fielded at corps level under direct Army command. However, the authorisation to use *Pluton* rests with the President. There are five operational regiments with at least 42 launch units equipped with *Pluton*, and these are supported with logistics, infantry protection and HQs.

The replacement system for the *Pluton*, known as *Hadès*, of which there are understood to be 15 units, are in store. The *Pluton* has a range between 17 and 120km, with a Circular Error Probable (CEP) of 164 to 341m. It is 7.64m in length and 1.41m in span. The term CEP refers to the radius of the circle around a target within which there is a 50 per cent probability that the warhead will fall. This means that the *Pluton* will land within 341m, at least, of its intended target after a flight of 120km, which is more than sufficient to destroy any target against which it is directed.

AMERICAN SYSTEMS – *LANCE* AND *PERSHING*

The American equivalent to *Pluton* was *Lance*, all of which have now been withdrawn from Europe. The Israeli Army still has 20 *Lance* missiles in storage. In its time *Lance* represented the standard NATO tactical nuclear support weapon. In the British Army there was one regiment with 12 launchers, the Italians and Belgians each had one battalion with six launchers and the then West German Army had four battalions each with four launchers. *Lance* was first test-fired in 1965. Production commenced in 1971, and it entered service with the US Army in the same year. The *Lance*, transported on a converted tracked M752 transporter, could be fitted with either a conventional or a nuclear warhead, and was always under dual-key launching arrangements with the US Army. The nuclear warhead such as the M234 could be fitted to produce a yield of 10, 50 or 100kt. *Lance* had a range of between 4.8 and 70km with a CEP of 455m.

The *Pershing* II missile, which carried a selectable yield nuclear warhead of between 5 and 50kt was deployed to Europe for a short while in the 1980s, but was withdrawn after the conclusion of the INF Treaty in 1987.

(right) **American-built *Lance* tactical nuclear missile, formerly deployed by several NATO countries**

(below) ***Lance* tactical nuclear missile on its transporter launcher**

Russian-built *Scud* missile with launcher vehicle

Launch of American-built *Pershing* II tactical nuclear missile; used only by American forces and now withdrawn under the 1987 INF Treaty

SOVIET SYSTEMS – *FROG* AND *SCUD*

The Soviets also deployed a number of tactical missile systems, such as the *FROG*-7 (Free Rocket Over Ground), which was transported on a fully self-contained ZIL-135 TEL vehicle. This early tactical nuclear support weapon had a range of between 15 and 65km, and carried a warhead with a 30 to 40kt yield and a CEP of 710m. The rocket could be made ready to fire in only 30 minutes and could be fitted with a chemical warhead in place of its nuclear warhead. This was replaced in service by the more reliable and accurate SS-21 missile with a range of at least 120km and which could be fitted with chemical or nuclear warheads. It is 9.44m in length and has a diameter of 460mm.

The *Scud* is probably the best known Soviet missile. There are a number of different types of *Scud* in service around the world, many of which have been modified by the purchasing state. For example, Iraq has modified some to the locally known *al Hussein* version, which has a range of 600km. Iraq had fired *Scuds* against the Iranians during their war and a further 93 were launched against Saudi Arabia and Israel during the Gulf War. The unmodified *Scud*-B can be fitted to carry either a chemical or a nuclear warhead with a yield of 40 to 100kt. It has a range of 280km with a CEP of 1,000m, which is quite inaccurate when compared with either French or American systems. A *Scud*-B fitted with a 100kt nuclear warhead would damage an area some 1,000m in radius.

NBC PROTECTIVE SYSTEMS

The close-toleranced components in the British S10 respirator have been developed to give a lightweight yet sturdy construction to provide the wearer with comfort over prolonged periods; here it is worn by a rating in the Royal Navy

British soldier using British-designed Mk.1, No.1 detector kit; note old-style S6 respirator

For every problem there is a solution, but in the case of something as complicated as NBC warfare it is not as straightforward as one would like to think. The way to survive in an NBC environment is actually twofold, each way of which enhances the other and increases battlefield survivability. The first point is the detection of toxic substances which must be made in advance, because to be forewarned is to be forearmed. Secondly, comes protection, which is the means through which an individual will survive an attack by chemical or biological weapons and the after effects of radioactive fallout from a nuclear attack. This protection is in the form of a personal protective suit and respirator, backed up by self-administered medication taken either orally or intramuscularly.

An individual on the battlefield has to have the means of protecting himself against the three actions which chemical agents have: killing, damaging and incapacitating. The first thing a soldier must do is have faith in his protective equipment. As a senior British Army officer put it: 'There is less likelihood of battle fatigue, casualties or mass "gas hysteria"... if soldiers have confidence in their NBC equipment and can operate it correctly.' In fact, it is widely accepted that troops operating in an NBC environment are more likely to suffer from the effects of stress than under normal combat conditions.

In the 1980s each Soviet soldier was known to be issued with a protective suit and respirator and a personal decontamination kit which also contained antidotes to both Soman and hydrogen cyanide. However, a protective suit is not the easiest garment in which to operate machinery or conduct even the simplest of tasks, such as driving a vehicle. As a result of tests conducted by the Soviets, they concluded that even in normal temperature ranges a man's performance may be reduced by as much as 50 per cent after wearing an NBC protective suit for several hours. These conclusions were upheld by NATO experts. Indeed, the Soviets even produced a chart with timescales attached to it recommending time limits in particular ranges. For example, at temperatures of 86°F an individual should ideally spend no longer than 20 minutes in an NBC suit. At temperatures of less than 59°F a soldier can operate for up to three hours in a suit. These were optimum times and longer operational periods could cause a man to

British troops firing an 81mm mortar; they are wearing Mk.3 NBC suits and S6 respirators

Medical team of US Army suited up ready to treat patients under NBC conditions; they are standing in front of a specially designed inflatable hospital with air filtration systems; only the man on the right has correct protective rubber overboots

collapse. However, theory never emulates practice, and in reality a man could find himself encapsulated in his NBC suit for several hours at a time, which was certainly the case during Operation DESERT STORM.

When the first gas attacks were mounted by the Germans during the First World War in 1915, they were the only belligerent nation prepared to operate under such conditions. This was only natural, because using such agents when one's own side was ill-equipped would not make for sound tactics. Even so, the first respirators (gas masks) were still only rudimentary affairs comprising gauze pads compressed and secured in place by straps which passed around the back of the head. The Germans were the first, again, to introduce special gas masks with either glass or mica eyepieces and an integral filter system to allow the wearer to breathe. The Allies were caught completely unprepared but soon set to devising their own respirators, such as the facelet mask made for the French Army by Dr Detourbe in 1915. Even then the eyes were left uncovered and French troops used goggles to protect their eyes. Other designs, such as the early British sets, were classed as anti-gas helmets and resembled cloth sacks with eyepieces set in them. The breathing vent had to be held between the wearer's teeth and the open end tucked into the collar of the tunic. Eventually respirators known as 'box sets' were

developed and these became the standard design, with most troops being issued with some form of gas mask by the end of the war. In future all troops would be issued with respirators.

In the late 1930s it became obvious that war in Europe was imminent. Germany was rearming and breaking virtually all the limitations placed on it by the Treaty of Versailles, thereby causing great concern throughout Europe. In Britain, for example, a nationwide issue of gas masks to the civilian population was undertaken. All were required to carry these with them everywhere and at all times, so great was the fear of poison gas being used in war. Even new-born babies were provided for by special hand-operated, bellows-type respirators. They were never popular, but considered to be better than nothing. Troops were issued with gas masks, but these had not improved greatly since the designs of 20 years earlier. In the event poison gas was never used in a strategic offensive, although it was held in reserve by Allied forces in most theatres in the event that Axis forces should resort to using it first.

Gas mask drill for US troops at Camp Callan (1950s); note exposed hands and rudimentary covering, which would not afford protection against nerve agents

The antidotes to chemical and biological agents and post-nuclear attack may be either self-administered or given prophylactically, that is to say taken in advance as a defensive measure. Vaccines may be administered to troops as an inoculation if the threat of biological warfare agents is considered high. This was the case during Operation DESERT STORM when thousands of American troops were vaccinated against anthrax.

Vaccines against biological agents may take one of three forms: they may be an attenuated form of the infective agent; an inactivated preparation of the virus or bacterium; or detoxified toxins produced by a micro-organism. These are designed to stimulate the production of protective antibodies within the body. For the most part these vaccines produce no side effects, but should any develop they are generally confined to mild irritation at the site of the injection and some mild fever and nausea. Only very rarely does a fatal side effect develop.

Three of the main anti-biological vaccines are intended to protect against botulinum, anthrax and plague. Each of these vaccines is backed up by anti-biotic BAT-TABS, or Biological Agent Treatment Tablets Set. These are taken by the soldier as a booster to the biological vaccines.

The botulinum vaccine is prepared from a growth of *Clostridium botulinum* which produces a type A toxin, which is inactivated by formaldehyde treatment and the resultant toxoid absorbed on aluminium hydroxide. Treatment is in three stages: the initial injection followed by a second two weeks later and the third ten weeks after the second. Side effects are not common but erythema and oedema may occur but subside after 48 hours at most.

The anthrax vaccine is prepared from a growth of the *Strene* strain of anthrax bacillus which has been rendered sterile by filtration processes, and contains 0.005 per cent w/v of thiomersal as a preservative. The anthrax vaccine is administered intramuscularly into the deltoid muscle in four doses of 0.5ml. The first three doses of the vaccine have to be given at three-weekly intervals backed up by the fourth injection after six months. Reactions may include mild erythema or swelling, but these last for only two or three days.

The plague vaccine, USP, is administered in a sterile formulation containing formaldehyde-killed whole bacilli (*Yersinia pestis*). It is administered into the deltoid muscle in three separate doses backed up by a fourth after six months. The first injection is 1.0ml of plague vaccine USP which is followed within three months by the second dose, but reduced to 0.2ml. The third injection of the same dosage is administered within six months of the second. Any reactions to the injections usually lessen 48 hours after administration. Due to the time lapses between the initial treatment and the boosters, it is understandable why the vaccines for biological agents must be given in advance.

Anti-nerve agent treatment is also twofold. The first element is Nerve Agent Protection (NAPS) tablets which a soldier can start to take before operating in an area where there is a high risk that chemical agents will be used. The second element comprises injections which must be self-administered by the soldier if he believes he has been affected by a chemical agent. The injection is in effect an antidote, designed to combat the biochemical effects of the nerve agent.

The NATO-approved standard for a self-administering injection comes in what is termed an auto-injector. These devices are about the size of a pen and are spring-loaded syringes which are pre-filled with the required antidote. This may vary slightly from one country to another but all have the same intended effect. The auto-inject system features a 20-gauge needle, which has been deemed not to be sufficient to compromise a soldier's NBC suit when used. For example, the

Old-style atropine injector being used to inject against chemical agents; it was always used in the upper thigh for quick response

A range of auto-injectors as used by NATO countries

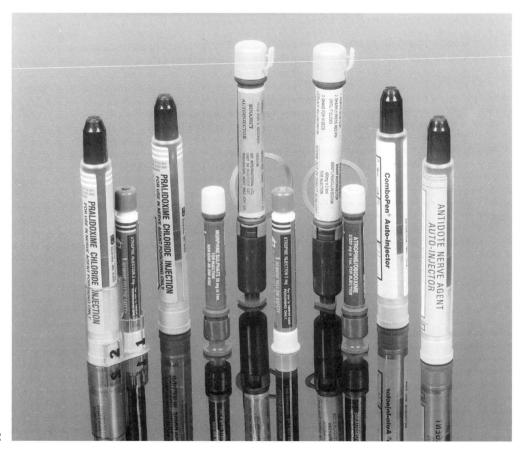

Canadian Army uses a single-chamber auto-injector containing 2g atropine sulphate and 22mg obidoxime chloride in 2ml. The specially developed Binaject is a twin-chambered auto-injector which incorporates the latest in state-of-the-art wet/dry systems. The system allows a soldier to treat either himself or a contaminated colleague. The Binaject contains 2mg of atropine sulphate in 2.4ml solvent, and 500mg of HI-6 powder. Other medications, including morphine, may be administered in this way.

The Russians may or may not have a similar system in operation, but the old-style method required a soldier to remove a cap to expose the needle on a special pre-filled capsule. This method required the man to think about what he was doing, although any revulsion he may have had about sticking a needle into his leg would certainly have disappeared in the trauma of battle. The autoject method does not require the soldier to consider what he is doing and thereby reduces his reluctance to inject himself. Atropine, oxime, NAPS and BATS are universally accepted antidotes to chemical and biological agents. Nemical-5 and potassium iodate are seen as the standard treatments for individual radiation contamination.

Soviet-style M10M respirator and L-INBC suit worn by infantryman injecting atropine chemical agent antidote

Decontamination kit with autoject devices as issued to the French Army

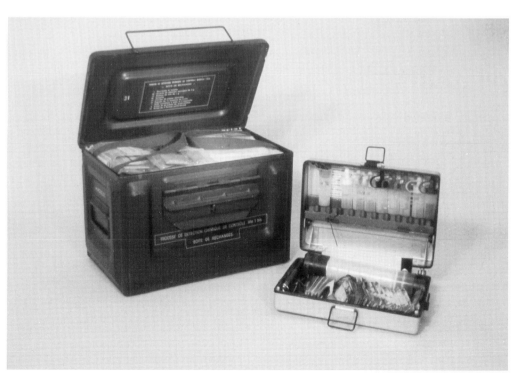

Respirators are issued to every man and woman on joining the armed forces. A female soldier who served with the Coalition forces during DESERT STORM recalls: 'You'd get this sickening feeling and your stomach would lurch when suddenly you'd go past a camp or another truck and everyone would have on their gas masks and NBC suits, and you didn't.' There are even reports of troops during the operation actually going to sleep while still wearing their respirators.

(left) **US Army NBC suit with full head respirator; note the rubberised overboots**

(right) **Close-up view of the British Army's old-style S6 respirator**

(bottom right) **Old-style S6 respirator in close-up; this man is wearing the Mk.3, No.1 suit**

BRITAIN – S6 AND S10

There are a number of designs of respirator in current service, each with its own characteristics. The current design in use with the British Army is the S10, which has all but replaced the older S6. A model called the S8 was found to be unsuitable and never entered service.

The British S10 is a full-face style secured by adjustable straps. It is fitted with two coated polycarbonate lenses which provide the wearer with a good field of view. The filter canister may be fitted to either side of the mask to facilitate equipment use by left- or right-handed operators, including infantrymen firing their rifles. A special integral drinking facility has also been built into this design and a speech module

incorporating a horn-loaded transmitter is also available. Low speech attenuation with good intelligibility and a microphone attachment for amplification make this respirator a good all-round design which is both comfortable and easy to wear. The S10 also allows the wearer to handle both personal weapons and crew-served weapons and operate night-vision equipment.

There are set drills for changing the filter canisters of the respirator, to avoid contaminated air or droplets

(left) **The latest S10 respirator as used by the British Army; the British Ministry of Defence has now selected the S10 to equip all branches of the armed services**

(right) **Typical style of NBC filters for respirators; these are of French design and clearly show the threaded ends for quick attachment to the respirator**

(below) **The complexity of the S10 respirator may be seen in this exploded view of its components**

of a chemical agent being introduced inadvertently into the respirator during the changing process:

1. Locate position of new canister and ensure that it can be grasped immediately;
2. Close the eyes and stop breathing;
3. Unscrew the old canister and discard it;
4. Screw on new canister as quickly as possible;
5. Blow out hard;
6. Thoroughly decontaminate gloves, exterior face-piece and canister;
7. Report incident to local commander.

Note that at no time does the soldier remove his respirator during the changing process.

(right) **Close-up view of the British Army's latest respirator design, the S10; it features a drinking system and may be fitted with voice communicators**

(below) **An historical range of respirators showing how the design has developed through the years; at the right is a First World War 'hood' design with a Second World War design next to it; to the left is the latest S10 respirator as used by the British Army; second from left is the S8 design which never entered service**

RUSSIA – MM-1, 41-M, M10M

The Russians have at least four designs in current service: the MM-1, 41-M (based on a design from the

(top left) **Operator wearing Soviet-style TEG-57 chemical de-contamination spray**

(top right) **Soviet-style 41-M respirator being worn by an infantryman; he is carrying his NBC suit in the stowed position on his back**

(bottom left) **Close-up of Soviet-style M10M respirator**

(bottom right) **Close-up of Soviet-style M10M respirator**

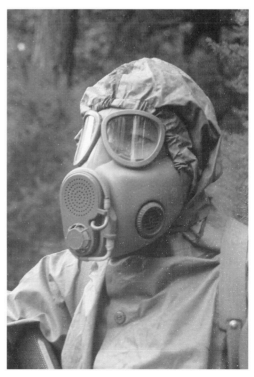

Second World War), the M10M (virtually a copy of the American M10 design) and a special version for tank and APC crews with flattened eyepieces to allow night-vision goggles and other optical equipment to be used while wearing the mask. The MM-1 utilises a trunk-like breathing tube terminating in a filter box which gives it a very old-fashioned appearance. The face mask is an over-the-head design which may produce a claustrophobic effect on some troops. As with other designs, it has two eyepieces to allow the wearer the best visual effects. The 41-M is another old design and is probably scheduled for replacement in frontline use. In NATO armies respirators have multi-purpose eyepieces. The latest Russian design is the M10M which is very advanced in design and would appear to be an all-purpose mask, probably to replace the older models.

(left) **Soviet-style Sch/Ms respirator worn with tank commander's helmet**

(bottom left) **Soviet-style respirator with tank commander's helmet and binoculars**

(bottom right) **Soviet-style 41-M respirator being worn by an infantryman taking shelter under a temporary anti-chemical protective sheet**

ISRAEL, FRANCE AND AUSTRIA

During the long-range bombardment of Israel by Iraqi *Scud* missiles, when chemical and biological attack was feared, respirators went on sale to the general public. These commercially available respirators were comparable to service-issue models. However, civilians untrained in their use sometimes panicked and hyperventilated, with at least one recorded death where the wearer omitted to remove the protective plastic seal from the filter unit. Normally Israel is not a frontline contender for NBC warfare (their *Merkava* tank does not have an NBC pack), but the troops are issued with

(right) **Diagram of the Turkish Army's SR6(M) respirator; it is also issued to the other services; it weighs 830g and provides 99.999% protection in an NBC environment which may contain a variety of agents; the diagram shows the method of operation of the filter, which contains artificial cellulose fibres**

(bottom right) **A British Army infantryman wearing the old-style S6 respirator in a low-threat environment**

(bottom left) **Soviet-style M10M respirator worn with L-I NBC suit with hood and rubber gloves**

respirators and regularly practise with them.

The French Army has several designs of respirator in current service, ranging from those for infantry and those specifically for the crews of armoured vehicles. The level of protection offered by the respirators' filtering system depends largely on the level of contamination, but on average may be up to several hours. The Austrians have developed a belt-worn respirator which

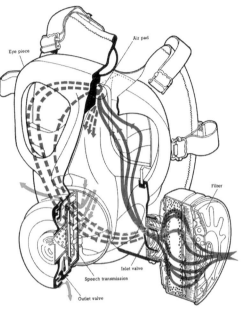

is battery operated and can provide the wearer with a completely closed system. It will deliver up to 300 litres of air per minute to the wearer to permit him to conduct even the heaviest of tasks. Known as ventilating equipment, this system offers the wearer complete comfort even at high ambient temperatures.

SPECIAL PURPOSE RESPIRATORS

Special closed systems based on self-contained, underwater breathing apparatus have been developed for bomb-disposal units, such as the British Army Royal Engineer units. These systems are worn by ordnance disposal operators when dealing with chemical munitions.

(below) **The M-95 NBC respirator currently in service with the Finnish armed forces; it weighs 500g, without the filter, and contains 50 separate components, including the filter, which weighs 259g; the filter will protect the wearer against all common agents for more than 48 hours with little if any deterioration in breathing rate; it is possible for the wearer to wear spectacles and a water-drinking facility will allow for the consumption of up to 0.25 l/min. The M-95 has a six-point head fixing harness to prevent slipping and the mask can be fitted in less than 10 seconds. It will perform equally well in temperatures as low as -40°C and as high as +40° C and still provide protection against biological, radioactive and chemical agents**

(top left) **British Army Royal Engineers working on an unexploded chemical-filled bomb**

(right) **The S3P NBC suit as issued to the French Army**

(bottom) **British Army Royal Engineer fully suited to work on an unexploded chemical-filled bomb**

61

Opposite

(left) **French Army tank driver's NBC coverall**

(right) **One of several types of chemical protective system and respirator issued to the French armed forces**

(bottom) **Fully-suited British Royal Engineers clear a path through a minefield under NBC conditions**

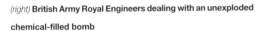

(right) **British Army Royal Engineers dealing with an unexploded chemical-filled bomb**

(bottom) **British Army Royal Engineer investigating a chemical bomb on an exercise; he is fully suited and is using special detection papers to determine the presence of chemical agents**

(top left) **British Army Royal Engineers suit up for disposal of an unexploded chemical-filled bomb; note air cylinder on man's back; both have respirators fitted**

(top right) **British Army Royal Engineers suit up to deal with an unexploded chemical-filled bomb**

(bottom left) **British Army Royal Engineers suiting up to deal with unexploded chemical-filled bomb**

(bottom right) **The S3P NBC suit as issued to the French Army**

(top) **British Army Royal Engineers bomb-disposal team in full NBC suits and respirators**

(bottom left) **British Army Royal Engineers suit-up to deal with unexploded chemical-filled bomb**

(bottom right) **British Army Royal Engineers suiting-up to deal with unexploded chemical-filled bomb**

British Army Royal Engineers dealing with chemical-filled mines under NBC conditions

French Army-style NBC protective suit and respirator

As with respirators, there are many types of NBC protective suits in current service. Some types have been developed specifically for a specialised task, such as bomb disposal, aircraft maintenance or medical services. Some designs rely on polymer-based materials, others on activated charcoal or in some cases rubberised materials. A typical polymer-based material from which NBC suits are manufactured will provide a barrier against the chemicals most likely to be encountered, such as mustard gas, for periods of up to 48 hours.

A fully NBC-suited RAF serviceman assembling a fuse for a 1,000lb bomb under NBC conditions; training is essential for such tasks

A soldier's personal NBC protection suit usually comes as a two-piece garment – trousers and jacket with integral hood. Only specialised units are usually provided with a one-piece garment. This protective suit is worn over the normal combat uniform and the webbing equipment is worn over the NBC suit.

Even those countries which are non-aligned, such as Switzerland, Sweden and Austria, all have a requirement to issue their troops with NBC protection, on the basis that it may be needed despite assurances that weapons of mass destruction will not be used.

The British Army uses a two-piece NBC suit which is donned by first pulling on the trousers which are fitted with straps to pass over the wearer's shoulders and then

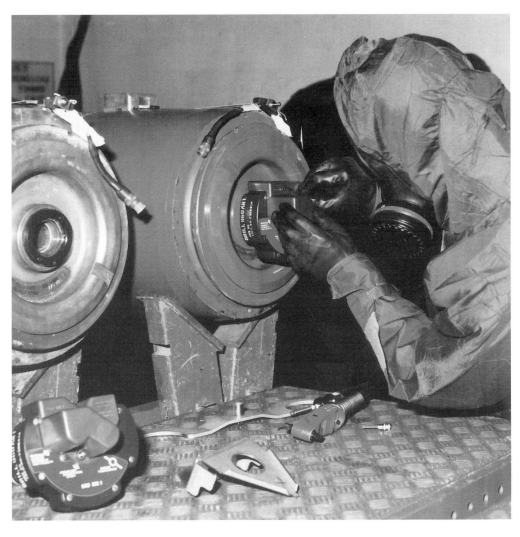

This page

(bottom left) **NBC protection, gloves and respirator as used by the Swedish Army**

(bottom right) **General view of the British Army's Mk.3 NBC suit and S6 respirator**

secured like braces. The jacket is an over-the-head garment which eliminates the need for front zip fastenings. This item is fitted with drawstring and Velcro fastenings. Special rubberised overboots are worn over the normal combat boot, and butyl rubber gloves, with separate cotton liners, complete the suit. The soldier would then put on his respirator, which in an emergency would be donned in one swift movement while he shouts 'Gas! Gas! Gas!' in an effort to expel any toxic substances which may be lingering inside the mask. The

British infantryman wearing the old-style Mk.3 NBC suit and S6 respirator

The British Army Mk.3 No.1 NBC suit

integral hood of the jacket is then drawn over the head and fitted around the rim of the respirator. Provided that the soldier does not panic, he is then protected against the effects of most if not all likely chemical and biological agents and residual radiation.

Repeated training scenarios prepare the soldier for operating in full NBC conditions, during which CS is sometimes used to create a sense of urgency and an atmosphere of realism. Wearing an NBC suit has been likened to 'going into battle with one hand tied behind our backs'. As can be appreciated, the wearer's body temperature will increase and his breathing become more laboured. Even a simple task such as aiming a rifle becomes much more difficult.

Protective suits for specialists operating in NBC conditions tend to be very complicated and require additional help to put them on properly in a co-operative 'buddy-buddy' manner.

Highly impermeable, multi-laminar polymeric films of only 0.1mm thickness have proved sufficient protection against chemical agents in vapour, liquid or powder form, and NBC suits manufactured from such materials would provide complete protection. The British Army at present has the Mk.4 suit and this meets current NATO standards. It is manufactured from non-woven materials which have absorption rates greater than those of anti-gas fabrics used in earlier suits. This is only the latest stage to which this type of suit has been taken, and an ongoing improvement programme will keep this level of defensive measure ahead of toxic developments.

For use in low-risk areas, but where chemical attack

is a possibility, an individual can wear a facelet mask. Several countries have these items in service and troops can use them where the risk is not high enough to warrant the wearing of respirators. These facelets are disposable and are worn in a manner not unlike a surgical mask, with fully-adjustable elasticated straps to secure the mask to the face. They are light enough for a soldier to carry two or three.

(right) **British soldier wearing the Army's latest NBC suit, the No.1 Mk.4 in Disruptive Pattern Material (DPM) material; he is also wearing the S10 respirator and the nylon-based Personal Load Carrying Equipment (PLCE), which is much easier to decontaminate because it does not readily absorb moisture or oil-based chemicals**

(bottom) **Sequence of how 'suiting up' with the old Mk.3 NBC suit was achieved**

(top left) **The British Army's latest NBC suit, the No.1 Mk.4, undergoing development trials**

(top right) **British Army Mk.3 No.1 NBC suit and S6 respirator**

Opposite

(top) **The latest Mk.4 No.1 NBC suit as used by the British Army; it is in DPM pattern and is fully functional with telecommunications and the latest S10 respirator**

(bottom) **NBC facelet mask for use in areas with low risk of NBC contamination**

(bottom) **Testing NBC suits and respirators for comfort under physical exercise in a controlled laboratory environment; the wearer's breathing and metabolism will be monitored to measure stress and performance**

The protection of vehicle crews has also been given high priority, and few designs of armoured fighting vehicles enter service without NBC protection. This facility comes in many forms, but in essence comprises the sealing of the vehicle and the creating of an overpressure to isolate the compartments of the vehicle; this is the design used on the German Army's *Leopard* tank series. For the most part these vehicle NBC packs are mounted in the turret where they are easy to maintain and the filtration system may be periodically replaced. Some larger command vehicles have a central filtration system into which individuals may plug themselves by means of umbilical breathing tubes. Some older vehicle designs, such as the Swedish S-Tank and Pbv 302 and the Dutch YP-408 do not have NBC facilities, but they could easily be retro-fitted.

(top) **A vehicle commander's respirator with headset and voice communication; it is based around the British Army's S10 respirator; voices are clear and distortion of verbal commands is minimal**

(bottom) **US troops undergoing field training in NBC warfare conditions**

Troops being transported around the battlefield in armoured personnel carriers, such as the British *Warrior*, the American *Bradley* M-3 or the M113, would be protected from NBC conditions by the vehicles' on-board protection pack. However, they would also be wearing their own personal protective suits and respirators to allow them to function as infantry when they left the vehicle to engage in combat. The Russians also use

this method and other nations are known to be seeking similar capabilities for their troops.

SHIPS AND AIRCRAFT

The other branches of the armed forces must each be aware of NBC warfare and its effects. Ships are considered to be collective protection environments by virtue of the entire crew, who must take steps to protect the ship against the effects of NBC attack by sealing off bulkheads and other compartment doors to prevent the spread of contamination throughout the vessel. They must also be prepared and equipped to decontaminate their equipment under such conditions. The Austrians are among a number of countries known to have developed a series of decontamination systems for use by their air force, comprising special sprays to deliver neutralising agents. Such special decontamination sets

may be used to spray fixed-wing aircraft and helicopters, to permit them to be used during a conflict. During the Gulf War the German Army could not for constitutional reasons take part in overseas missions, but to show their solidarity in supporting the Coalition they deployed a number of *Fuchs* APCs which had been specially modified to act in the role of NBC detecting vehicles.

(top) **French Army decontamination unit mounted on TRM 2000 truck**

(bottom) **The ultimate in collective protection centres. Naval vessels must be aware of NBC threats and ships such as this, the Royal Navy's HMS *Norfolk*, carry a comprehensive range of protective systems for the crew; it is also capable of decontaminating itself by the use of seawater**

For major units such as field hospitals where large volumes of uncontaminated air are required, special NBC filtration units are available. These are portable units designed to provide toxin-free air for the protection of personnel in unhardened, collective, protective systems, such as inflatable hospital units. These hospitals, referred to as collective protective systems, are laid out to provide set-aside areas where a wounded man can be decontaminated and his NBC suit removed safely before he is moved into the treatment and ward area. Typically such a portable system will remove better than 99.9 per cent of toxic substances from the air.

For the treatment of the wounded in NBC conditions, several types of casualty bag with NBC filtration systems have been developed. The Austrians have the VBS 93 bag with NBC ventilating equipment SAB 87/2F. Two battery-powered ventilators will provide the injured soldier with filtered air for up to 20 hours before batteries or filters need replacement. The system is fitted with a large observation panel and carrying handles. The patient will be comfortable in this system for periods between four to eight hours, at the end of which he should – in theory at least – be stabilised and in proper treatment facilities.

The French Army has a similar system, but made in transparent material and inflated with decontaminated air. The wounded soldier is placed inside the transportation bag, which is part of a rig and resembles a stretcher to allow him to be carried. The base of the bag has at least four separate filter canisters of the standard respirator type. There are other variations on the basic design, some of which have extra filter

US Air Force medical personnel in NBC protective kit carry a man with simulated wounds from an ambulance under NBC exercise conditions

canisters and lifting handles.

For the walking wounded a series of body bags which envelop the upper torso are in current service. These systems enclose the trunk, head and arms of a soldier, feature a vision slit and are voluminous enough to permit the soldier to continue wearing his respirator if it has not been damaged.

Other medical facilities developed for use in NBC

(top) **American soldier erecting an inflatable medical centre for the treatment of troops under NBC conditions; this man is inserting the air filtration unit**

(bottom) **NBC medical bag for transporting wounded troops; note filter pack at foot of bag, lifting straps and observation panel over man's face**

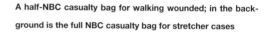

(top left) **French Army transport bags for injured troops under NBC conditions**

(bottom left) **Ambulances would be used by the army to transport the wounded under NBC conditions; this one is based on the Land Rover but not equipped with an NBC pack**

A half-NBC casualty bag for walking wounded; in the background is the full NBC casualty bag for stretcher cases

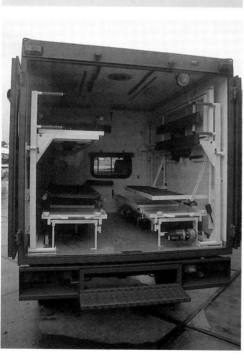

environments include activated-charcoal cloth anti-bacterial field dressings and the French-developed Protection, Individual Nerve Gas (PING) individual dressing. This special dressing sachet acts on most wounds contaminated by toxic chemicals, including VX and G agents. The kit is supplied with a double-faced, absorbent glove fitted with a fastening of Velcro for the wrist. The person applying the dressing uses the glove to eliminate most of the chemical poisoning in the injured area and applies sterilising/decontaminating agents, supplied in the kit, to the wound. The absorbing pad which forms the dressing is applied to the wound site and secured by tape. These dressings weigh only 230g

and are of small volume, which means that an individual can carry two or three of them.

Working conditions for medical personnel are very hazardous and stressful when operating under full NBC conditions; not only do they have to protect the wounded but also maintain their own personal defences and the integrity of their NBC suits and respirators. Wounded troops would be transported in AFVs which have dedicated roles, such as the British Army's *Samaritan* which is one of the range of *Scorpion* AFVs; these vehicles all feature NBC packs for the protection of the crews.

(right) **An anti-bacterial field dressing with activated charcoal as part of its composition; this would be invaluable to troops under NBC conditions**

(bottom) **Treating a patient under full NBC conditions; this is a British Army exercise and the men are wearing S10 respirators and using what appear to be ordinary toilet brushes to apply fuller's earth to decontaminate the injured man**

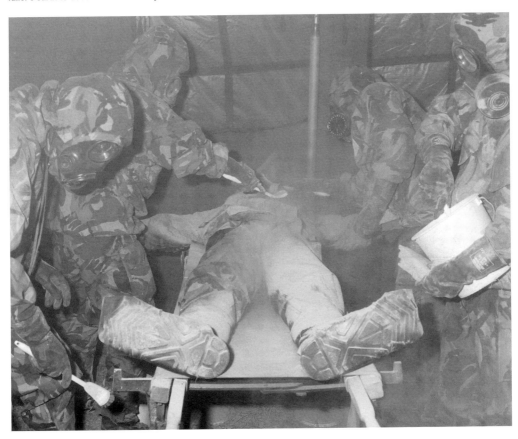

(left) The *Samaritan* armoured ambulance of the British Army; it is an unarmed version of the *Scorpion* and is fitted with a pack to permit full operation under NBC conditions

(below) Training medical staff to treat wounded troops under simulated NBC conditions; these are members of the British Royal Army Medical Corps. If this were a real incident there is probably little they could do to save this man because his respirator is smashed

Personal decontamination kits are issued to every soldier when entering a combat zone where the likelihood of chemical attack is considered high. These kits are compact enough to fit into a pouch of the soldier's personal kit. For the most part, decontamination by the individual is based on nothing more complex than sachets or puffers of fuller's earth, which is highly absorbent. The soldier can apply fuller's earth to the contaminated part with impregnated pads or the puffers. Once the chemical agent is absorbed, the process of decontamination is made much easier.

For advance warning of airborne chemical sprays the British Army issues sets of detector paper strips which a soldier applies to points on his NBC suit. The paper is specially treated and changes colour if a toxic vapour is present.

(bottom left) **Infantryman holding a Soviet-style chemical-agent detector kit; he is wearing an L-I NBC suit**

(right) **Transdermal patch under development to replace the orally-taken NAP tablet; this acts by releasing its agent over a 24-hour period**

(bottom right) **Detail of how fuller's earth is used to decontaminate a Mk.3 NBC suit**

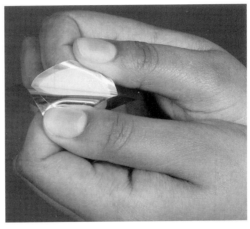

NATO forces also have the decontaminant agent XLIEI, which is applied with a simple pump and may be used to decontaminate small vehicles and unit equipment. The Russian Army has the TEG-57 spray tank carried by one man for decontaminating individuals affected by chemical agents. This device is worn on the back and operates by hand-pumping the pressure chamber to allow the decontaminating liquid to flow in

aerosol form. A pack containing scrubbing brushes and replenishment liquids completes the system. Decontamination of personal webbing equipment has been made much easier with the introduction of nylon-based materials which do not absorb moisture, unlike the old canvas-type materials.

The Russian Army is highly organised in the field of NBC defence and known to have specialised chemical reconnaissance and defence units for detecting the agents, marking out areas which are contaminated, and vehicles with equipment for mass decontamination. At least 17 different types of vehicle have been identified as being for NBC defence, including the BRDM-rkh which carries 40 warning flags which are automatically emplaced to warn of contaminated areas. Another vehicle is the TMS-65 decontamination vehicle which features a VK-1F turbojet mounted on the chassis of a 6x6 Ural-375E truck. This vehicle is used in the decontamination of large objects such as radar sets, tanks and vehicles.

At the height of the Cold War a typical Soviet NBC Defence Battalion would hold on strength at least 16 ARS 14 trucks each of which held a reservoir of 2,750

(left) **Preparing the Soviet-style TEG-57 chemical decontamination spray for use**

(bottom) **British decontaminant chemical agent XLIEI which is discharged by means of a simple hand pump; this powder may be used to decontaminate small vehicles, unit equipment and personnel**

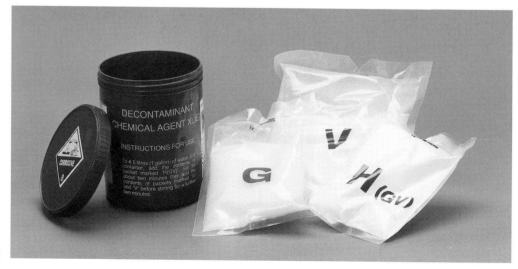

litres of decontaminating liquid, and the DDA-53 vehicle was also available to them. These were scaled at the rate of six to the divisional NBC battalion and one for the regimental NBC company. These vehicles used steam with decontaminating liquids to treat clothing and smaller items of equipment, such as personal weapons. Even today, there is no reason to believe that such high level priorities are not still in place for NBC warfare in the Russian Army and other former member states of the Warsaw Pact.

Some NATO forces have high-pressure hoses to spray wash contaminated vehicles, and shower facilities for decontaminating troops in the field. Even commercially available high-pressure spraying equipment which has been 'militarised' may be brought into use.

(right) **Soviet-style 41-M respirator being worn by an infantryman sheltering under temporary personal chemical protection sheet**

(bottom) **The Soviet TEG-57 chemical decontamination unit in use to spray an infantryman**

(left) **Preparing the Soviet TEG-57 chemical decontamination spray for use**

(middle) **Soviet truck-mounted model ARS-12 decontamination unit in operation during an NBC exercise; this may be used to decontaminate smaller vehicles and equipment**

(bottom) **Soviet model TMS-65 decontamination unit in operation, cleaning main battle tanks during an NBC exercise**

(top left) **British troops using a hand-held spray to decontaminate a** *Warrior* **AFV; note the use of 'low-tech' equipment in the form of a bucket; this is not uncommon and many ordinary items may be used for NBC decontamination**

(top right) **French Army high-pressure decontamination spray for use in cleaning vehicles under NBC conditions**

(bottom) **A British AFV, a** *Challenger* **repair and recovery vehicle, emerges from a test facility; such trials are conducted to test the NBC protection pack**

(top) French troops use high-pressure decontamination sprays to clean an AMX-30 vehicle armed with *Roland* anti-aircraft missiles

(bottom) French Army ACMAT VMTH 1000 decontamination kit mounted on a TRM 2000 lorry

Water-filtration system for purifying large volumes under NBC conditions

Pure drinking water is an essential element in any environment and under NBC conditions its supply and storage become crucial. First, a water supply must be sampled and the British have developed the No.2 Mk.1 device for detecting the presence of poisons. It is a simple but reliable method of testing for the presence of agents such as cyanides, mustards, heavy metals and nerve agents. A full range of individual water filtration systems has also been developed to protect against water-borne biological agents such as cholera and typhoid. Larger, motor-powered filtration systems, capable of delivering between 2,700 and 23,000 l/hr have also been developed. These are towed by vehicles and will treat water supplies contaminated with NBC agents to better than 99 per cent purity. This is achieved by using filter systems which have been pre-coated with diatomaceous earth which will remove particulate solid matter with diameters as small as one micron.

The British-designed and built NBC6 filtration unit for decontaminating drinking water in an NBC environment

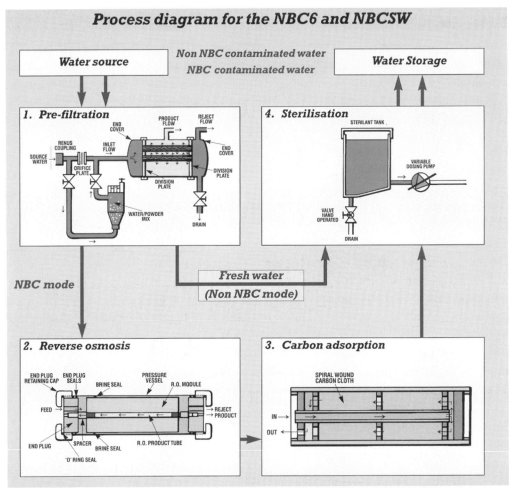

Process diagram for the NBC6 and NBCSW

Water source

Non NBC contaminated water

NBC contaminated water

Water Storage

1. Pre-filtration

END COVER
PRODUCT FLOW →
REJECT FLOW
RENUS COUPLING
INLET FLOW →
SOURCE WATER →
ORIFICE PLATE
END COVER
DIVISION PLATE
DIVISION PLATE
WATER/POWDER MIX
DRAIN

4. Sterilisation

STERILANT TANK
VARIABLE DOSING PUMP →
VALVE HAND OPERATED
DRAIN

NBC mode

Fresh water

(Non NBC mode)

2. Reverse osmosis

END PLUG RETAINING CAP
END PLUG SEALS
BRINE SEAL
PRESSURE VESSEL
R.O. MODULE
FEED →
→ REJECT
→ PRODUCT
END PLUG
SPACER
BRINE SEAL
R.O. PRODUCT TUBE
'O' RING SEAL

3. Carbon adsorption

SPIRAL WOUND CARBON CLOTH
IN →
OUT ←

(top) **Diagram to illustrate the workings of the NBC6 water-filtration unit**

(bottom) **The British-designed and built SW water-filtration unit for use in an NBC environment; this will deliver up to 1,900 litres of clean drinking water per hour from a contaminated saline source**

As mentioned earlier, illnesses resulting from exposure to chemical agents continued to be reported long after the end of the First World War. The same pattern followed the American withdrawal from Vietnam, during which conflict a number of servicemen were exposed to 'Agent Orange'. This was a defoliant chemical, but it was contaminated by the herbicide 2,4,5-trichlorophenoxyethanoic acid (2,4,5-T) which is believed to have caused long-term genetic disorders.

In the few years since Operation DESERT STORM ended troops have complained of a range of symptoms which have come to be referred to as Gulf War Syndrome. The reported symptoms include chronic fatigue, listlessness, low sperm count, nausea and headaches. The precise cause of these effects remains a mystery. It is generally accepted that chemical and biological agents were not used during the conflict, although some sources dispute this. However, defence agencies are now accepting that organophosphates, highly effective pesticides, were used in greater quantities and more widely than was at first believed. The theory is gaining ground that some of the symptoms of 'Gulf War Syndrome' may be due to exposure to these organophosphates. Defence agencies remain divided, but the Americans accept that Gulf War Syndrome exists and have recorded about 45,000 cases.

During DESERT STORM about 51,000 British service men and women were deployed, of which about a thousand have reported illnesses of the Gulf War Syndrome type. This figure is much lower than the American one, but still constitutes two per cent of the total British commitment. However, at the time of writing, the British Ministry of Defence does not officially recognise the malaise. Medical reports have been compiled on 80 per cent of the total number of reported cases, but because of the range of symptoms being reported diagnosis is not straightforward. The symptoms described are not physically visible, and it is impossible to rule out the possibility that they may be psychosomatic. There is also the problem that some soldiers may be reluctant to report such symptoms, for fear of damaging their military career prospects. The Ministry of Defence has invited the Medical Research Council to act as an independent body to investigate the cases and make proposals.

89

Predictions of future trends in operational roles on the battlefield suggest an increase in specialised combat systems being developed for improved troop survivability. Infantrymen will have special combat suits incorporating lightweight body armour for protection against small arms fire, as well as fire-resistant materials. The combat suit could also incorporate an integral NBC protection system. The helmet would be an all-in-one design, not unlike some current designs of motorcyclists' helmets which have rise-and-fall visors. This style of helmet would have an in-built NBC filtering system, thereby eliminating the need for a separate respirator. Each man would carry individual NBC treatment packs, containing atropine and oxime, and a repair kit should his suit's integrity be harmed by accidental tearing during operations.

The French are known to be investigating such a comprehensive combat system, with input from several leading defence manufacturers, and the British have studied a similar design too. However, the price of equipping each soldier with such a specialised NBC-proof combat suit would be prohibitively high. This leads one to conclude that only troops deployed with special Rapid Reaction Forces would be issued with them. Such troops would be the most likely to find themselves operating in a region with a high risk of NBC contamination. The technology is already available to produce such a comprehensive combat system, but it is a question of cost versus necessity.

The development of better and continuously improved NBC protection is a never-ending struggle to increase the infantryman's survivability under the most hazardous conditions. Battle fatigue under such conditions would be a high risk and, to make provision for this, special rest area installations have been developed. A typical design would incorporate at least two high-capacity NBC filtration systems feeding into an air conditioning unit to provide overpressure air to a toxin-free area. Troops passing from this area would first put on their NBC suits and pass into an inner airlock and then exit to the outside by a second airlock. Entrance would be effected in the reverse manner to maintain the integrity of the system.

(top) **French future combat system; is it possible that future NBC suits will be multi-purpose in design like this?**

(bottom) **The future infantryman? This was put together by several British companies in the early 1980s; it has clearly influenced the comparable French project, which is in an advanced state of development and incorporates an integral NBC protective system**

Britain has renounced its chemical and biological warfare capability, and has instead turned its facilities at the Chemical Biological Defence Establishment (CBDE), Porton Down over to developing NBC defence. The scientists at Porton Down develop NBC protective equipment and vaccines. At present Porton Down is developing a transdermal patch to replace the need to take NAPS tablets orally. This patch is similar in action to anti-smoking nicotine patches, and releases its dose over 24 hours. Other systems being developed there include self-decontaminating surfaces for vehicles.

It is a constant struggle to maintain a lead in defeating toxic agents. If they get it right everyone will thank them for their efforts. If they get it wrong there may be few around to complain.

(right) **French Army NBC suit for use in tropical conditions**

(bottom) **Versatile portable filter unit designed by the CBDE, Porton Down, and used to supply clean air under NBC conditions to collective protection systems such as medical centres**

British troops crew an 81mm mortar; they are wearing S10
respirators and Mk.4 No.1 DPM pattern NBC suits

DETECTION AND EARLY WARNING SYSTEMS

British soldier using the hand-held chemical agent monitor; he is wearing the S10 respirator and has attached chemical agent detector papers to his lower arms and upper legs as a back-up should the CAM fail

As stated in the previous chapter, protection against NBC warfare is enhanced by the detection of such toxic agents on the battlefield. Such detection is of as much importance to the troops on the ground as radar and sonar are to the air force and the navy. In the early days of gas warfare small animals, such as canaries and mice, were used to give advance warning. With a metabolic rate some 15 times faster than that of humans, canaries were frequently used in deep mines to warn the miners of the presence of gas, and in warfare they served a similar role.

In the trench systems of the First World War, spent shell cases were hung up on poles and were struck when the presence of gas was suspected. Other methods of early warning included wooden gas rattles, which were rotated in a manner similar to that used by football supporters. Shouting in a loud voice also served to alert troops to the presence of gas. Indeed, this last method still has a bearing on today's battlefield if a soldier observes a low-flying aircraft trailing a plume of vapour behind it. This may sound a rather hit or miss method, but it is preferable that a false alarm should be raised than that one should be caught unprepared by an undetected real attack.

Battlefield NBC detection systems are available in three forms: hand-held, crew-served and remote stand-alone. They range from being almost primitive in form to state-of-the-art systems incorporating technological advances in electronic detection.

British soldier fully suited for operating in an NBC environment; he is wearing an S10 respirator and holding a small camera on a boom arm with a light unit for investigating confined spaces

British soldier using a chemical agent monitor to check a Land
Rover for chemical contamination

British No.1 Mk.1 detector kit for vapour agents

British No.1 Mk.1 detector kit for chemical agents; it is compact enough to be worn on a belt in its self-contained pouch or clipped to a soldier's webbing ready for immediate use

The British Army's detector kit, chemical agent, residual vapour, No.1 Mk.1 is issued at the rate of one each to section commanders and is meant to be used in the event of an attack where a chemical agent is believed to be present. The kit is contained in a small fold-away pouch and carries all the necessary equipment for conducting sampling of the atmosphere. It has four bottles with reagent capsules, 32 sampler tickets and a hand pump which is simply squeezed to take in an air sample. The reagent capsules are activated to moisten the sampler tickets and the hand pump is operated. The reagent changes colour according to the agent present and the operator can check this reaction off against the set of samples contained in the instruction list. This method may seem unsophisticated, but it has been proved workable.

The Russian Army also has a hand-operated system, but theirs is more comprehensive than the British one. This device uses a series of sealed glass tubes which are opened before being inserted into a hand-

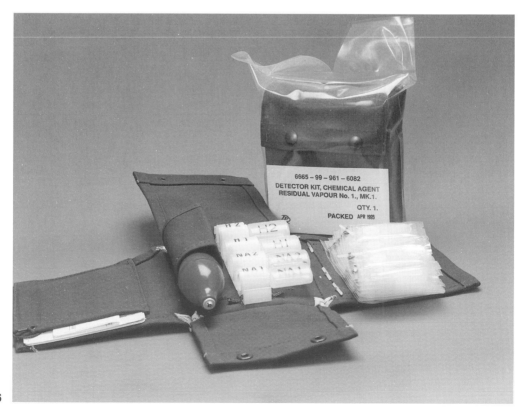

held device. The reagents in the tubes react in a similar manner to the treated paper, and the operator reads off the type of agent present and its concentration level. This equipment is contained in a metal case and carries everything needed by the operator to detect chemical agents locally present.

(right) **The use of specially-treated, chemical-agent detector paper; this was developed in Britain and has been supplied to other NATO forces**

(bottom) **British No.1 Mk.1 detector kit for chemical agents; note old-style atropine injectors**

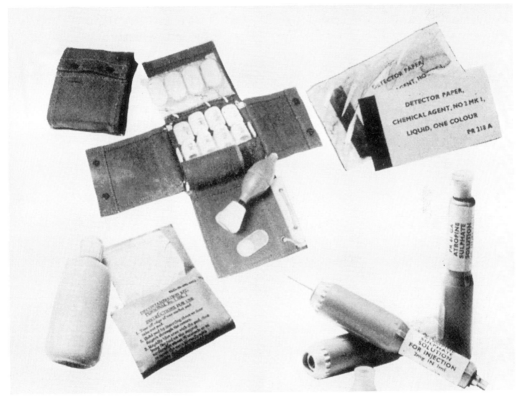

(top) **The British chemical agent monitor**

(bottom) **View of the *Fuchs* AFV supplied by the German Army for use in Operation DESERT STORM; it is fitted with the British CAM device above the headlights**

The hand-held Chemical Agent Monitor (CAM), developed for the British Army, is an example of high-technology NBC detection. It is presently in use with about 20 countries including several branches of the US forces. During the Gulf War it was in widespread use with the Coalition forces. The German-supplied

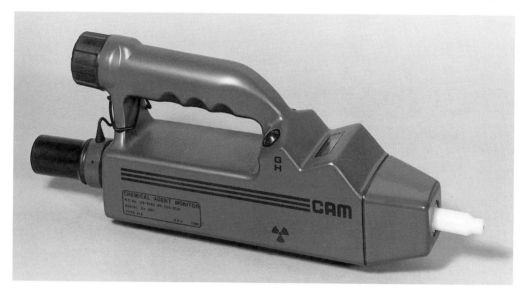

Fuchs (Fox) was dedicated to NBC detection with a CAM mounted above the headlights on either side of the vehicle. It was this device which was used to check the impact sites of *Scud* missiles for the presence of chemical agents.

The CAM uses ion-mobility spectrometry principles to respond selectively and accurately to the presence of chemical agent vapours. In use, the CAM draws an air sample into the unit where it is ionised by a weak

(top) **The British chemical agent monitor, which is in widespread use; it is light, easy to use and simple in operation; these devices were fitted to the *Fuchs* armoured vehicles supplied by the German Army during Operation DESERT STORM**

(bottom) **Using a simulator chemical agent monitor to familiarise British troops with its use under NBC conditions**

(top) **The Japanese Ground Self-Defense Force chemical protection and detection vehicle, based on a 6x6 wheeled chassis. This armoured vehicle serves in the same role as the German *Fuchs*; however, this design carries a more comprehensive array of chemical warfare protective systems, including early warning and 'sniffer' devices**

(bottom left) **British soldier using the CAM; note that he is wearing nylon-based webbing which reduces contamination risk and is easier to decontaminate when exposed to a chemical agent**

(bottom right) **Close-up of the CAM monitoring device as fitted to the *Fuchs* AFV during Operation DESERT STORM**

radioactive source. The molecules of the agent are characterised by their ability to form low-mobility ionic clusters and these are classified according to their mobility relative to a known vapour source. The CAM contains an in-built microcomputer which indicates the level of toxicity present.

The CAM is easy to use and simple to operate, with low false alarm rates – an important factor for troops operating in NBC conditions. The controls of the device comprise an on/off push button and a mode change switch. One-handed operation of the device is considered to be normal operating procedure. The CAM itself may be easily decontaminated and it is rugged enough to withstand normal military wear and tear.

There are a number of stand-alone or remote sensor alarms available for detecting the presence of chemical agents. One such device is the American XM-21 Remote Sensing Agent Alarm, which is mounted on a tripod, but may be emplaced by one man. This device is capable of detecting clouds of nerve and vesicant agents at ranges of over 5km, to give ground troops plenty of warning and permit them to take the necessary protective action.

A similar British device is known as the Nerve Agent Indicator Automatic Detection (NAIAD), which is also a

stand-alone, remotely-operating nerve agent detector. Remote sensors available with this device, which weighs 14kg, may be emplaced out to 700m from troop locations.

The M90 Chemical Warfare Agent Detector from Finland is light enough and sufficiently compact in design to allow it to be used as either a stand-alone remote device or to be operated by one person. The M90 will sound an alarm in less than ten seconds after detecting any chemical agent, but the level of concentration detected may be altered to suit conditions. It has a low false alarm rate and can be interfaced with local command, control and communication systems to provide a comprehensive chemical alerting system.

The GID-3 and GID-2A have been developed for the specialised roles of armoured warfare and warships, respectively. The GID-3 Chemical Agent Detection System uses Ion-Mobility Spectrometry (IMS), like the hand-held CAM device, but is used to detect the threat of chemical agents outside a vehicle. It can monitor the collective protection of the crew compartment and confirm the effective operation of the filter system to support the vehicle's on-board NBC protection pack. The GID-3 may also be removed from the vehicle and set up

Function of the chemical agent monitor

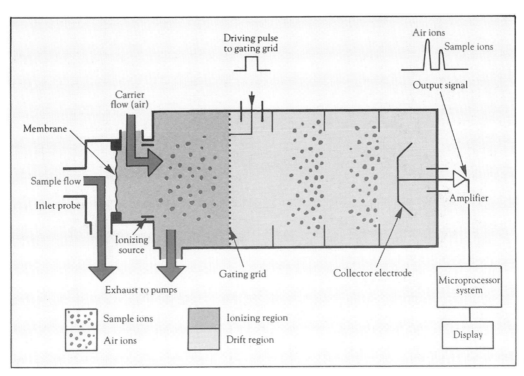

as a remote sensing point to integrate into a network supplying early warning to a central display console.

The GID-2A system operates in a similar manner but has been designed specifically to support maritime operations. The GID-2A has a low false alarm rate and, like other devices in the range, may be integrated into a centralised display and control system located in the ship's damage control centre. An extended role for the CAM is to incorporate it into the Field Alarm Monitor (FAM) to serve as a local sentry alarm. It will monitor the presence of blister and nerve agents in the usual manner, and continue to monitor for the presence of such agents after an attack. By providing a localised report it

The American-designed XM-21 Remote Sensing Agent Alarm which is a stand-alone device mounted on a tripod; it is capable of sensing nerve and vesicant agent clouds at distances greater than 5km

allows the local commander to make the decision on whether it is safe or not to remove respirators. This obviates the need for units to contact a centralised command unit, which itself may be experiencing a chemical attack.

Nerve Agent Mode (G) selected
Instrument in warm-up phase

Nerve Agent Mode (G) selected
Relatively low concentration indicated (2 blocks visible)

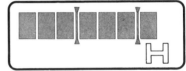

Blister Agent Mode (H) selected
Relatively high concentration indicated (7 blocks visible)

Battery Low Indication (BL)

(top right) **CAM mode displays**

(top left) **The M-90 chemical agent monitor which may either be used stand-alone or integrated into a detection network**

(bottom left) **The British Army's NAIAD nerve agent detector; this can be used as a stand-alone alerting device or networked into a comprehensive NBC alerting system**

(top) **A remote chemical-sensing monitor as used by the French Army**

(bottom left) **The British GID-2A device for detection of chemical agents on ships or airfields; it may be integrated into a C³I network**

(bottom right) **The British GID-3 chemical agent monitor for use in armoured fighting vehicles and ships; it may also be utilised as a stand-alone remote sensor unit**

Where there is the risk of radioactive contamination a whole range of detection systems has been developed in a programme which often parallels the nuclear power industry – for example, the wearing of personal dosimeters to indicate the level of radiation absorbed over a period of time. Such devices could be made available to individual troops operating in an area where a nuclear device had been detonated.

A number of specialised suits have also been developed with enclosed breathing systems to allow operations in an environment contaminated with radioactive particles. Interestingly, the Russians have developed a one-piece suit and boots which have copper wire woven into the material. The exact purpose of this is unknown – there is no known scientific evidence that copper used in this way will protect against radiation.

The British-designed Portable Dose Rate Meter

PDRM 82M serves as a good example of a typical device intended for an irradiated environment. It is a lightweight, portable, gamma-radiation survey meter designed to measure the radiological dose rate in the range of 0.1 to 300 centigrays per hour. Results are processed through a microcomputer chip, and the readout is displayed as easily-understood figures on a liquid-crystal display.

Detection methods have come a long way since the days of canaries and mice. As with the development of protective systems, research on detection cannot afford to stand still. Indeed, a continuous improvement and development programme is in place around the world. This is not just to safeguard military personnel but also civilians. When the Chernobyl nuclear power station went 'critical' in Ukraine in April 1986, a radioactive cloud passed over densely populated areas of Western Europe

Soviet-style MM-1 respirator; the wearer is measuring the height of the cloud following an atomic explosion and gauging the force of the blast

Soviet-style anti-radiation suit; it is bulky but hard-wearing to protect against short-term exposure, showing details of boots, hood and gloves

and contaminated sheep in certain areas of England and Wales – to the extent that even in the mid 1990s they are still regarded as unfit for consumption. This illustrated how vulnerable everybody is – military and civilian alike - to the invisible effects of radiation.

Soviet-style anti-radiation suit, showing detail of hood and front-fastening zipper

The ICAD miniature chemical agent detector which may be worn by an individual to monitor for the presence of agents when operating beyond other networked monitoring systems

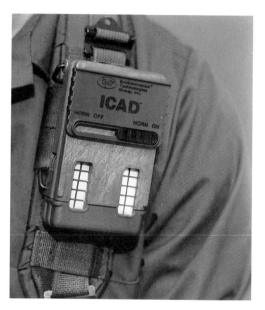

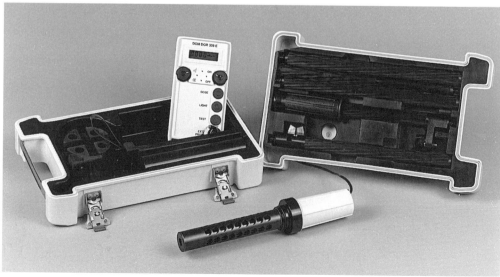

French Army hand-held DOM DOR 309 NBC detection unit

THE FUTURE OF
NBC WARFARE

With the end of the Cold War and the collapse of the Warsaw Pact it was considered imprudent to maintain such high levels of troop concentrations in Europe. Between 1989 and 1990 negotiations were conducted in Vienna. Levels of conventional (that is, non-nuclear) forces in Europe were agreed upon and subsequently the so-called 'Open Skies' Treaty was concluded. In 1987 the USA and the Soviet Union had agreed upon the INF Treaty regarding the elimination of nuclear missiles with ranges between 500 and 5,500km. This took into account more than 300 American cruise missiles and some 120 *Pershing* II missiles, but not battlefield weapons; the treaty led to the removal of approximately 220 SS-12 and 167 SS-23 Soviet missiles. Subsequent negotiations between the USA and the Soviet Union such as the Strategic Arms Reduction Talks (START) have eased global tensions to the point where nuclear conflict between them is now only a remote possibility.

However, more and more countries around the world are working towards a nuclear weapons capability. As smaller, sometimes belligerent, nations obtain a nuclear capability, there is a growing risk that the threat, or even use, of nuclear weapons may be used to settle disagreements. As long ago as 1974, India detonated a nuclear device in what was undoubtedly a demonstration to other nations in the region, particularly Pakistan, that it had the ability to strike with nuclear weapons.

Unsuccessful attempts were made to include the British and French nuclear deterrent in the arms reduction talks and today these independent strike forces remain in place unaffected by arms reduction talks. However, these two countries are scaling down their nuclear arsenals of their own accord, with France understood to be dismantling its missile silos on the Plateau d'Albion and Britain relinquishing tactical weapons and free-fall bombs, although still retaining the *Trident* SLBM. Considering the implications of using their nuclear strike forces, it seems unlikely that either Britain or France would resort to their use without consultation. Other nuclear nations, such as China and India, might prove more difficult to bring to the negotiating table.

A pre-emptive strike to set back a potential enemy's nuclear programme is always a possibility. Such a strike was carried out by Israel in June 1981, when it mounted a series of air raids against the *Osirak* nuclear power station just outside Baghdad. It was feared by Israel that Iraq would use this facility to produce weapons-grade material to construct a nuclear device. The raid was

Foreign observers watch the destruction of Soviet chemical weapons; diplomats and military experts from 45 countries examine weapons to be decommissioned, October 1987

successful but highly criticised at the time. The fact that Israel itself is considered a prime candidate for constructing and delivering a nuclear weapon is sometimes overlooked.

Test-ban treaties to stop nuclear testing in the atmosphere, underwater or underground have been put in place, but in the past such agreements have been broken. At least nowadays there are sophisticated methods of detecting when a nuclear test has been carried out. Seismic monitoring and satellites, for example, have made it easier to monitor nuclear testing.

There will always be someone – whether nations or terrorist groups – keen to acquire nuclear devices by fair means or foul. Since the breakdown of the Soviet Union, the West has put considerable resources into monitoring scientists from the former Warsaw Pact, who might be tempted to sell their services to corrupt regimes. There is known to be a small but thriving black market in weapons-grade nuclear material. These issues are outside the scope of this work, but they do highlight the fact that, while the nature of the nuclear threat has changed dramatically in recent years, the danger has certainly not gone away.

Chemical and biological weapons testing remains virtually impossible to monitor. Chance plays a key part, as at Sverdlovsk in 1979, where a satellite happened to monitor the effects of what was later proved to be an outbreak of anthrax.

Allegation and counter-allegation of 'dirty tricks' abound during war. Between 1979 and 1983 Meo tribesmen who had fled from Laos accused Pathet Lao and Vietnamese troops of using chemical and biological weapons against them. During its involvement in Afghanistan the Soviet Army was accused of using chemical warfare against the hill tribesmen, and this accusation was once more levelled against them when they used gas against rioters in Georgia. Georgian toxicologists later confirmed that nerve gas had been used, but the Russians insisted the agent was harmless tear gas.

Back in the 1960s, the superpowers co-existed through

Soviet operators lift the empty case of a chemical air bomb out of the discharge chamber where the agent was drained from the weapon at Shikhany, Saratov Region, 4 October 1987; the process was observed by experts from 45 countries

mutual deterrence, although they could have destroyed the world many times over. At the time, the nuclear strategist Albert Wohlstetter summed up the situation by stating that the world lived in 'a delicate balance of terror'.

Today, it is no longer the major powers which are the threat with nuclear, chemical or biological weapons. It is more likely that an emergent nation wishing to make a powerful statement would use a weapon of mass destruction. With the involvement of UN armed forces in conflict zones around the world, soldiers of any nationality could still find themselves called upon to fight in an NBC environment.

A more frightening prospect still is that of organised crime or terrorist groups holding the world to ransom with the threat of unleashing a nuclear, biological or chemical attack against a civilian target – a prospect that, ironically, has been brought closer by the ending of the Cold War.

Foreign observers inspect the chemical weapons to be destroyed at the Shikhany military base in the Saratov Region, 4 October 1987

British experts and Soviet and foreign newsmen visit the chemical training centre in the Moscow region on 30 June 1988; this was a return visit by British experts after an earlier visit by Soviet observers to Porton Down; the soldier in the left foreground is wearing a Hungarian-style, type 70M respirator

Adams, James, *Trading in Death: The Modern Arms Race.* Hutchinson, London (1990).

Compton, James A F, *Military, Chemical and Biological Agents.*

Winter, Dennis, *Death's Men.* Penguin Books, London (1978).